The Future of Healthcare Subsidies
Navigating Changes in the Affordable Care Act

BY
Birtle Abrams

CONTENTS

INTRODUCTION 1

Part 1: 10
The Foundation – Understanding Healthcare Subsidies and the ACA 10

Chapter 01 11
The Affordable Care Act and Its Original Vision 11
Chapter 02 22
The Basics of Healthcare Subsidies 22
Chapter 03 33
Navigating the Healthcare Marketplace 33

PART 2: 44
The Changing Landscape – What's New in Subsidies 44

Chapter 04 45
COVID-19 and Its Impact on Healthcare Subsidies 45
Chapter 05 56
The Inflation Reduction Act and Its Impact on ACA Subsidies 56
Chapter 06 66
State-Specific Changes to Healthcare Subsidies 66

Part 3: 77
Maximizing Your Healthcare Benefits 77

Chapter 07 78
Maximizing Your Healthcare Benefits 78
....78
Chapter 08 88

Choosing the Right Health Insurance Plan for You 88
Chapter 09...99
Special Considerations: Families, Seniors, and the Self-Employed...99

Part 4: **110**
The Future of Subsidies and What Lies Ahead...........110

Chapter 10...111
Policy Shifts: What to Expect in the Coming Years.......111
Chapter 11...122
How to Appeal Denials or Subsidy Adjustments 122
Chapter 12...133
The Future of ACA and Healthcare Subsidies: Looking Ahead 133

Conclusion **145**

INTRODUCTION

Understanding the Evolving Landscape of Healthcare Subsidies

Healthcare has always been a topic of significant importance in the United States. For millions of individuals and families, accessing affordable care has been a constant struggle, and despite efforts from various stakeholders, the system has remained complex and difficult to navigate. Enter the Affordable Care Act (ACA), a landmark piece of legislation passed in 2010, designed to provide greater access to affordable health insurance, expand Medicaid, and make healthcare more inclusive and affordable for Americans, especially those with low to moderate incomes.

Overview of the Affordable Care Act (ACA)

The Affordable Care Act, commonly known as Obamacare, was introduced to address the gaps and disparities in the U.S. healthcare system. At its core, the ACA aimed to make healthcare more affordable and accessible for all, including those who had previously been unable to secure health insurance due to pre-existing conditions or unaffordable premiums.

One of the most significant components of the ACA was the establishment of health insurance exchanges, commonly known as the *Marketplace*. These online platforms allow individuals and families to shop for health insurance plans that meet certain minimum standards, with the added benefit of subsidies to help make coverage more affordable.

Subsidies are essentially financial assistance provided to individuals and families based on their income level, ensuring that those who need help can access coverage that would otherwise be too expensive. These subsidies can significantly lower the cost of premiums and out-of-pocket expenses for medical care, making healthcare more affordable for those who need it most.

Recent Changes and Why They Matter

While the ACA was revolutionary in its time, healthcare needs and economic conditions evolve, and the law has undergone a series of changes over the past decade. Perhaps most notably, the COVID-19 pandemic triggered a surge of temporary enhancements to the ACA's subsidy provisions. The *American Rescue Plan (ARP)* passed in 2021, provided expanded eligibility for subsidies, significantly increasing financial assistance and even extending subsidies to individuals who had previously been excluded due to earning more than 400% of the federal poverty level (FPL).

This was followed by the *Inflation Reduction Act (IRA)* in 2022, which extended these enhanced subsidies through 2025. These legislative changes have dramatically increased access to affordable healthcare for millions of Americans, leading to lower premiums and a reduction in the number of uninsured individuals.

However, these changes also created new challenges. With the expiration of some temporary provisions on the horizon, many individuals may find themselves in a position where they no longer qualify for certain subsidies or face higher premiums. Understanding these shifts and preparing for what's next will be crucial for anyone relying on the Marketplace to secure coverage.

As we move into a new era of healthcare policy, it's essential to stay informed and ready to make smart decisions that align with your evolving needs. This guide aims to provide you with the necessary tools and insights to navigate these changes confidently.

Purpose of the Guide: Empowering Individuals, Families, and Professionals to Navigate Subsidy Changes

This guidebook has been created to help you understand the current landscape of healthcare subsidies under the Affordable Care Act, focusing on the changes that have occurred in recent years and what they mean for your health insurance options. Whether you're an individual trying to navigate the complexities of the healthcare system, a family seeking affordable coverage, or a professional working with clients in need of assistance, this book will give you the tools to understand and maximize the available subsidies.

Healthcare subsidies are crucial in ensuring that Americans have access to the medical care they need without being burdened by unaffordable costs. These subsidies are designed to make insurance premiums more manageable for individuals and families who fall within certain income brackets. With the right knowledge, you can leverage these subsidies to choose the best health insurance plans for your circumstances.

We understand that healthcare decisions can be overwhelming, especially with constant changes in laws and regulations. The goal of this book is to simplify these complexities by breaking down the changes in the ACA and offering clear, actionable advice. You'll find straightforward steps to determine your eligibility, how to apply for subsidies, and how to choose the best health plan to fit your needs.

Brief Explanation of Key Terms

To get started, it's important to understand some of the basic terms that will be referenced throughout this guide. While these may seem technical at first, we'll break them down so you can feel confident in your ability to navigate the ACA system.

Subsidies: Financial assistance provided to help reduce the cost of health insurance. Subsidies come in different forms, including premium tax credits and cost-sharing reductions.

Premium Tax Credits (PTC): These are subsidies that reduce the amount you pay for your monthly health insurance premiums. The amount of the credit depends on your household income and size.

Marketplace: An online platform where you can shop for and compare health insurance plans. The Marketplace is where you apply for subsidies and where you'll enroll in coverage through the ACA.

Cost-Sharing Reductions (CSR): These are subsidies that reduce your out-of-pocket costs, such as copayments and deductibles, for certain health plans purchased through the Marketplace.

Federal Poverty Level (FPL): A measure used to determine eligibility for various government assistance programs, including subsidies for health insurance. Your eligibility for subsidies is largely determined by where your income falls in relation to the FPL.

Understanding these key terms is essential, as they form the foundation of how the ACA works. With this knowledge, you'll be able to better navigate the Marketplace and make decisions that are in your best interest.

The Role of Healthcare Subsidies in Expanding Access to Care

One of the primary goals of the ACA was to increase access to healthcare for underserved and underinsured populations. Before the ACA, millions of Americans went without health insurance because they couldn't afford it or had pre-existing conditions that made coverage unaffordable. Healthcare subsidies play a critical role in achieving the ACA's mission by making health insurance plans more affordable for those who need them most.

Subsidies help bridge the gap for families and individuals who earn too much to qualify for Medicaid but too little to afford private insurance. By lowering monthly premiums and out-of-pocket costs, subsidies make it possible for millions of Americans to access necessary medical care. Without subsidies, many people would be left to choose between forgoing insurance altogether or paying premiums that they can't afford, leading to significant health and financial risks.

The expanded eligibility for subsidies introduced by the American Rescue Plan and extended by the Inflation Reduction Act has made it even easier for Americans to access affordable healthcare. These changes have lowered premiums for many people, even those who previously didn't qualify for assistance. As a result, more individuals are able to obtain quality healthcare, leading to better health outcomes, lower levels of financial distress, and fewer people forced into medical debt due to high medical costs.

How This Book Will Help You Make Informed Decisions About Healthcare Subsidies

This book will guide you through the complexities of healthcare subsidies, explaining the changes that have occurred under the ACA and how you can benefit from them. Whether you're currently enrolled in a Marketplace plan or considering enrollment for the first time, this guide will help you understand the options available to you and how to take full advantage of them.

Clarity: We will break down complex rules and jargon so that you can clearly understand what healthcare subsidies are available to you and how to apply for them.

Actionable Steps: We'll provide a step-by-step guide to help you navigate the enrollment process, including how to apply for subsidies, which health plans to consider, and how to ensure you get the best deal.

Preparation for Future Changes: We'll help you stay informed about future policy changes and give you strategies for adapting to shifts in subsidy availability or eligibility, including how to plan for potential increases in premiums or the expiration of enhanced subsidies.

Maximizing Your Benefits: We'll show you how to calculate your eligibility and choose the health plan that best fits your needs and budget, so you can maximize the value of the subsidies you receive.

This guide is here to help you make confident, informed decisions about your healthcare. By the end of this book, you'll not only understand how to navigate the ACA's subsidy system, but you'll also be empowered to advocate for your own healthcare needs, ensuring that you and your family have the coverage you deserve.

Final Thoughts

The world of healthcare subsidies is complex, but with the right tools, you can successfully navigate it. This book will provide you with the information you need to make the best decisions for your health and finances. The landscape is constantly evolving, but by staying informed and proactive, you can ensure that you have the support you need to get the coverage that fits your life. You're not alone in this journey—this guide is here to help you every step of the way. Let's dive in and explore how you can take control of your healthcare future.

Part 1:
The Foundation – Understanding Healthcare Subsidies and the ACA

Chapter 01

The Affordable Care Act and Its Original Vision

The Affordable Care Act (ACA), also known as Obamacare, was a monumental step in the history of U.S. healthcare reform. Passed into law in 2010, the ACA sought to address critical issues in the healthcare system, such as rising insurance premiums, lack of access to care, and health disparities among different segments of the population. The law was designed to increase the accessibility, affordability, and quality of healthcare, with particular attention to those who were previously left out or underinsured.

This chapter will dive into the birth of the ACA, its key provisions, and how it laid the groundwork for the subsidies that now help millions of Americans access healthcare. Understanding the original vision of the ACA will help you better appreciate the changes that have occurred since its passage and how those changes continue to shape the healthcare landscape today.

The Birth of the ACA: Key Goals and Promises

The Affordable Care Act was a direct response to the growing problem of millions of Americans who either lacked health insurance or could not afford adequate coverage. Before the ACA, approximately 50 million Americans were uninsured, and many more were underinsured, meaning their insurance didn't cover basic health needs or was unaffordable when they needed care.

The key goals of the ACA were ambitious:

Universal Coverage: One of the ACA's primary goals was to provide health insurance coverage to as many

Americans as possible. The law sought to reduce the number of uninsured individuals by making coverage more affordable and accessible.

Health Insurance Market Reform: The ACA sought to address problems in the insurance market, where insurers often denied coverage to people with pre-existing conditions, imposed lifetime coverage limits, or charged exorbitant premiums based on age or health status.

Lower Healthcare Costs: While the ACA did not fully address the skyrocketing costs of healthcare, it aimed to make it more affordable for individuals and families by providing subsidies and creating an organized marketplace to shop for plans.

Improving Health Outcomes: The ACA was also designed to improve health outcomes by expanding access to preventive care, ensuring people could seek care before conditions became severe, and providing coverage for essential health services.

Holding Insurers Accountable: The ACA introduced rules to prevent insurance companies from exploiting consumers, such as removing the ability to deny coverage based on pre-existing conditions and preventing lifetime or annual coverage caps.

By creating a more regulated and accessible healthcare system, the ACA aimed to reduce the financial burden of medical costs, promote healthier populations, and provide a safety net for the most vulnerable.

Major Provisions of the ACA

To achieve these goals, the ACA introduced several groundbreaking provisions that radically transformed the U.S. healthcare system. Below are some of the most important aspects of the law.

1. The Individual Mandate

One of the most controversial provisions of the ACA was the individual mandate, which required most Americans to have health insurance or pay a penalty. The goal was to encourage healthier individuals to enter the insurance market, helping to balance the higher costs incurred by those with pre-existing conditions or chronic illnesses.

Why it mattered: The idea behind the individual mandate was to ensure that the insurance pool was large enough to cover both healthy and unhealthy individuals. This would help keep premiums more affordable for everyone by spreading the cost across a larger group.

Changes: While the individual mandate was repealed at the federal level in 2017 (effectively eliminating the penalty for not having insurance), the requirement still exists in certain states, such as California, Massachusetts, and New Jersey.

2. Medicaid Expansion

The ACA aimed to extend healthcare coverage to more low-income individuals through an expansion of Medicaid. Medicaid, a joint federal and state program, provides coverage to those with limited incomes, but prior to the ACA, it was not universally available across all states.

Expansion: The ACA expanded Medicaid eligibility to include individuals earning up to 138% of the federal poverty level (FPL), providing healthcare coverage to millions of low-income Americans who were previously ineligible for Medicaid.

State Opt-Out: While the ACA offered expanded Medicaid to all states, the Supreme Court ruled in 2012 that states could opt out of Medicaid expansion. As a result, some states chose not to expand the program, leaving millions without access to affordable care.

3. Health Insurance Exchanges (The Marketplace)

Perhaps one of the most influential aspects of the ACA was the establishment of Health Insurance Marketplaces (also known as exchanges), which are online platforms where individuals and families can shop for health insurance plans. These exchanges are designed to make health insurance more transparent, allowing consumers to compare different plans and select the one that best fits their needs and budget.

Marketplace Options: The ACA created a federally-run Marketplace (HealthCare.gov), while some states created their own state-based marketplaces. These platforms offer a variety of health insurance plans that meet ACA requirements for essential health benefits.

Subsidies: Health Insurance Marketplaces are where individuals can apply for premium subsidies, which lower the monthly cost of premiums, and cost-sharing reductions (CSRs), which reduce out-of-pocket costs like deductibles, copayments, and coinsurance.

How Subsidies Work in the ACA System

Subsidies are at the heart of the ACA's approach to making healthcare affordable. There are two primary types of subsidies available to those who qualify: **Premium Tax Credits** (PTCs) and **Cost-Sharing Reductions** (CSRs).

Premium Tax Credits (PTC)

Premium tax credits are subsidies that lower the amount you pay for your monthly health insurance premium. The amount you qualify for depends on your income and the federal poverty level (FPL), as well as the cost of premiums in your area.

How it works: If your income is between 100% and 400% of the federal poverty level, you can apply for premium tax credits. These credits are based on a sliding scale, meaning the lower your income, the more financial help you will receive.

How to apply: You apply for premium tax credits through the Health Insurance Marketplace when you purchase a health plan. The amount of the subsidy will be calculated based on the information you provide, including your income, household size, and other relevant details.

Cost-Sharing Reductions (CSRs)

Cost-sharing reductions are another form of subsidy that lowers your out-of-pocket expenses. These reductions can help decrease the amount you pay for deductibles, copayments, and coinsurance.

How it works: Unlike premium tax credits, CSRs are only available to individuals who purchase a Silver-tier plan through the Marketplace and whose income is between 100% and 250% of the FPL. These reductions can make a significant difference in reducing overall healthcare costs.

How to apply: To qualify for CSRs, you must apply for them when you shop for coverage on the Marketplace. If you meet the income requirements, your CSR will be applied automatically once you select a Silver plan.

Eligibility Criteria for ACA Subsidies

The ACA's subsidies are designed to assist low- and middle-income individuals and families in affording health insurance coverage. However, not everyone qualifies for these subsidies. The eligibility for both premium tax credits and cost-sharing reductions depends on a few factors:

Income

Your eligibility for ACA subsidies is primarily based on your household income. The federal government determines eligibility by comparing your income to the federal poverty level (FPL), which varies by household size and is updated annually.

> **Income Range**: To qualify for premium tax credits, your income must be between 100% and 400% of the FPL. For cost-sharing reductions, your income must fall between 100% and 250% of the FPL, but you must also purchase a Silver plan to receive them.

Household Size

The number of people in your household is also important in determining your subsidy eligibility. The ACA takes into account the total number of people in your household and adjusts the FPL according to household size.

> **Example**: A family of four with an income of $100,000 may qualify for different subsidies than a single individual with the same income, depending on the family size and the subsidy rules for that year.

Citizenship and Residency Status

To be eligible for ACA subsidies, you must be a U.S. citizen or a legal resident. Undocumented immigrants are not eligible for subsidies under the ACA. However, legal immigrants may be eligible, provided they meet other requirements.

The Relationship Between Income, Family Size, and Subsidy Amounts

One of the key factors that determine the amount of subsidy you receive is your household income in relation to the federal poverty level. The ACA uses a sliding scale to determine how much you will pay for your health insurance premium, with those at the lower end of the income spectrum receiving the most assistance.

Income Below 100% of the FPL: For individuals who earn less than 100% of the FPL, they may qualify for Medicaid (if the state has expanded Medicaid under the ACA) or other forms of assistance. In some states that didn't expand Medicaid, these individuals may struggle to find affordable coverage, even with subsidies.

Income Between 100% and 400% of the FPL: This is the primary income range for ACA premium tax credits. As your income increases, the subsidy amount decreases, but it's still designed to keep premiums affordable.

Income Above 400% of the FPL: If you earn more than 400% of the FPL, you typically won't qualify for premium tax credits, although you may still be eligible for other forms of assistance, depending on your state.

The Impact of ACA Subsidies on Healthcare Affordability for Low- and Middle-Income Families

One of the most significant achievements of the ACA has been its impact on healthcare affordability, particularly for low- and middle-income families. Before the ACA, millions of Americans faced either unaffordable premiums or no access to coverage at all.

Affordable Coverage: With the introduction of subsidies, millions of Americans who were previously unable to afford health insurance gained access to necessary coverage. Subsidies reduce the financial burden of monthly premiums, and cost-sharing reductions lower the amount individuals and families pay when they access care.

Better Health Outcomes: By making healthcare more affordable, subsidies allow families to seek preventative care, manage chronic conditions, and access timely treatments—all of which contribute to better health outcomes and improved quality of life.

In summary, the ACA revolutionized the U.S. healthcare system by expanding access to care, particularly for low- and middle-income Americans. The subsidies provided under the law have played a central role in making health insurance more affordable for millions of individuals and families. By understanding how the ACA works and how subsidies are applied, you can better navigate the healthcare marketplace and make decisions that lead to better health and financial security.

Chapter 02

The Basics of Healthcare Subsidies

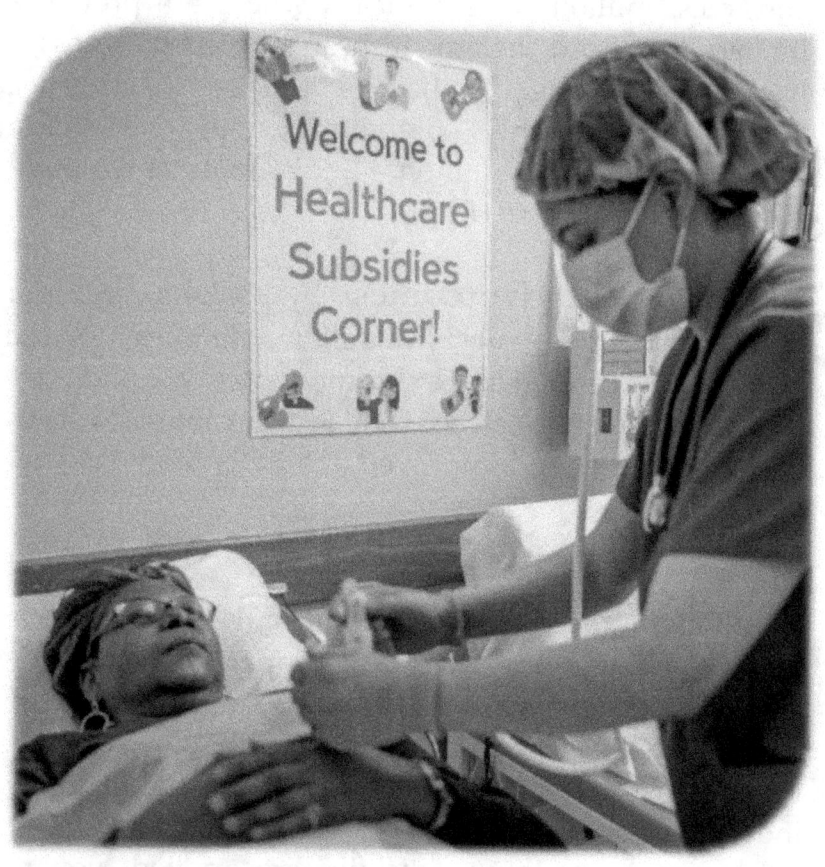

Healthcare subsidies are a cornerstone of the Affordable Care Act (ACA), designed to make health insurance more affordable for Americans. These subsidies help reduce the financial burden of purchasing coverage, particularly for individuals and families with low to moderate incomes. Whether you're looking to sign up for a health insurance plan through the Marketplace or are already enrolled, understanding the basics of healthcare subsidies is crucial to ensuring you get the best deal possible for your coverage.

This chapter will break down the different types of healthcare subsidies available under the ACA, explain how they work, and provide practical guidance on eligibility requirements and the application process. Additionally, we will discuss the concept of the "subsidy cliff" and its impact on families who fall just outside the subsidy range.

What Are Healthcare Subsidies?

In simple terms, healthcare subsidies are financial assistance programs designed to help individuals and families pay for health insurance premiums and reduce out-of-pocket healthcare costs. The ACA introduced subsidies to bridge the gap for individuals who earn too much to qualify for Medicaid but too little to afford private health insurance premiums on their own.

Without subsidies, many Americans would be unable to afford the cost of health insurance, leaving them uninsured or underinsured. Subsidies make coverage more accessible, ensuring that individuals and families can get the care they need without facing financial hardship. These subsidies are primarily available through the Health Insurance Marketplace (also called the Exchange), an online platform that allows individuals to shop for insurance plans that meet ACA standards.

Subsidies are typically designed to assist with two major components of health insurance:

> **Monthly Premiums**: The amount you pay each month to your health insurance company for coverage.
> **Out-of-Pocket Costs**: These are costs that you pay directly when you seek medical care, such as deductibles, copayments, and coinsurance.

By reducing both premiums and out-of-pocket expenses, subsidies ensure that individuals and families can access comprehensive health coverage while minimizing their financial burden.

Types of Subsidies: Premium Tax Credits (PTC) vs. Cost-Sharing Reductions (CSR)

There are two primary types of subsidies under the ACA: **Premium Tax Credits (PTC)** and **Cost-Sharing Reductions (CSR)**. While both subsidies aim to make healthcare more affordable, they target different aspects of the health insurance experience.

Premium Tax Credits (PTC)

Premium Tax Credits (PTC) are subsidies that reduce the amount you pay for your monthly health insurance premium. These tax credits are available to individuals and families who purchase coverage through the Health Insurance Marketplace and meet certain income requirements.

How it works: The amount of your Premium Tax Credit depends on your household income and size. If your income falls between 100% and 400% of the Federal Poverty Level (FPL), you qualify for PTC. The subsidy helps reduce the monthly cost of your health insurance premiums, making them more affordable.

Income Scale: The lower your income, the higher your Premium Tax Credit. This ensures that those with lower incomes receive more financial assistance. If your income is near 400% of the FPL, your PTC will be smaller, but it will still reduce the cost of your premiums.

Example: A single person earning $30,000 per year might receive a PTC that reduces their monthly premium from $500 to $200, making insurance far more affordable.

Cost-Sharing Reductions (CSR)

Cost-Sharing Reductions (CSR) are another form of subsidy designed to reduce your out-of-pocket costs when you use healthcare services. These reductions can lower the amount you pay for copayments, deductibles, and coinsurance.

How it works: CSRs are only available if you buy a Silver-level plan through the Marketplace. Silver plans offer a moderate level of coverage, and the CSRs make these plans more affordable for individuals and families with incomes between 100% and 250% of the Federal Poverty Level (FPL). CSRs increase the value of Silver plans by reducing out-of-pocket expenses like deductibles and copayments.

Income Range: To qualify for CSRs, your household income must fall between 100% and 250% of the FPL. The amount of cost-sharing reduction you receive depends on how low your income is within that range. For example, a family of four with an income of $40,000 might qualify for substantial cost-sharing reductions, significantly lowering their costs for doctor visits, hospital stays, and prescriptions.

Example: Without CSRs, a Silver plan might have a $3,000 deductible. With CSRs, that deductible could be reduced to $1,000, making healthcare more affordable when you need care.

How Subsidies Lower Monthly Premiums and Out-of-Pocket Costs

Subsidies directly affect both the monthly premium you pay for coverage and the out-of-pocket costs you face when receiving healthcare services.

Premium Tax Credits Lowering Monthly Premiums

> **Sliding Scale**: The amount of Premium Tax Credit you receive depends on your income and household size. If your income is closer to the poverty level, you'll likely qualify for more financial assistance.
> **Affordability**: PTCs ensure that health insurance premiums are affordable relative to your income. The ACA sets a cap on how much of your income can go toward premiums. Even if you're at the higher end of the subsidy range, you won't have to pay more than a certain percentage of your income toward your premiums.

For example, someone with a lower income might pay only 4% to 9% of their income for a health plan's premium, even if the full cost of the premium is higher. The Premium Tax Credit will cover the difference.

Cost-Sharing Reductions Lowering Out-of-Pocket Costs

While PTCs help make premiums affordable, CSRs focus on reducing the costs of accessing care. When you visit a doctor or get a prescription, you typically have to pay some portion of the cost (e.g., a copay or a deductible). CSRs reduce these costs, making it easier for people with lower incomes to access necessary care without financial strain.

Lower Deductibles: If you qualify for CSRs, your deductible for a Silver plan may be reduced. This can save you hundreds or even thousands of dollars in the event that you need to use your insurance.

Reduced Copayments: Copayments for doctor visits, prescriptions, and specialist care are also reduced for those receiving CSRs, making healthcare even more affordable.

Together, PTCs and CSRs provide a dual benefit: they lower the cost of insurance premiums, and they reduce the amount of money you need to pay when you seek medical care.

Key Eligibility Factors for Subsidies: Income Thresholds and Household Size

To qualify for healthcare subsidies through the ACA, your eligibility depends primarily on two key factors: **income** and **household size**. Understanding how these factors work together will help you determine whether you qualify for assistance and how much you could potentially receive.

Income Thresholds

The eligibility for both PTCs and CSRs is determined based on your household income as a percentage of the Federal Poverty Level (FPL).

Premium Tax Credits (PTC): To qualify for Premium Tax Credits, your income must be between 100% and 400% of the FPL. If your income is higher than 400% of the FPL, you will not be eligible for PTCs, although you can still purchase coverage through the Marketplace at full price.

Cost-Sharing Reductions (CSR): To qualify for CSRs, your income must fall between 100% and 250% of the FPL, and you must purchase a Silver plan through the Marketplace. Unlike PTCs, CSRs are not available for those with income above 250% of the FPL.

Household Size

The number of people in your household directly impacts your eligibility for subsidies. A larger household generally increases the income limits for subsidy eligibility.

> **Example**: A single individual with an income of $35,000 may qualify for a certain amount of subsidies, while a family of four with the same income would be eligible for different subsidy levels, with higher limits based on the larger household size.

To determine your eligibility, the Marketplace will ask for household information, including your income and the number of people living with you. It's important to report this information accurately, as your subsidies depend on these figures.

How to Apply for Healthcare Subsidies Through the Health Insurance Marketplace

The process for applying for healthcare subsidies is straightforward, but it requires careful attention to detail. To apply for subsidies, you'll need to:

Create an Account on the Marketplace: First, visit the Health Insurance Marketplace website

(HealthCare.gov) and create an account. You'll need to provide some basic personal information, such as your name, address, and social security number.

Complete the Application: The application will ask you about your income, household size, and other relevant information to determine your eligibility for subsidies. Be as accurate as possible when reporting this information to ensure you receive the correct subsidy amount.

Review Plan Options: Once you've completed the application, you'll be presented with a variety of health insurance plans available in your area. The Marketplace will also show you which plans qualify for subsidies and how much financial assistance you'll receive.

Choose a Plan and Enroll: After reviewing your options, select the health insurance plan that best meets your needs and budget. Once enrolled, you'll start receiving the subsidies that lower your monthly premiums and, if eligible, reduce your out-of-pocket costs.

The Impact of the "Subsidy Cliff" on Families with Income Above 400% FPL

The "subsidy cliff" is a term used to describe the sudden loss of subsidies for individuals or families whose income exceeds 400% of the Federal Poverty Level (FPL).

What is the Subsidy Cliff?: Once your income surpasses 400% of the FPL, you no longer qualify for premium tax credits. This means you could be paying full price for your health insurance premiums, which can be a significant jump, especially if you were previously receiving a substantial subsidy.

Example: If a family of four earns $120,000 per year, they may qualify for a premium tax credit if their income is below the 400% FPL threshold. However, if their income rises above this threshold, they would lose the subsidy and have to pay full price for their health plan.

This subsidy cliff has been a source of concern for many families, as it can create a sharp increase in the cost of coverage, making it financially difficult to afford health insurance. There have been calls for lawmakers to address this issue, but as of now, the cliff remains a significant challenge for families near the upper income limit for subsidies.

Conclusion

Healthcare subsidies are a vital part of the Affordable Care Act, making insurance more affordable for millions of Americans. Understanding the different types of subsidies, eligibility requirements, and how to apply for them can help you navigate the complex world of healthcare coverage. By taking advantage of these financial assistance programs, you can ensure that your healthcare remains affordable and accessible.

As you move forward with understanding healthcare subsidies, remember that the ultimate goal is to ensure that you, your family, or your clients have access to the healthcare they need without breaking the bank.

Chapter 03
Navigating the Healthcare Marketplace

Navigating the healthcare marketplace is one of the most important steps in securing affordable coverage under the Affordable Care Act (ACA). Whether you're a first-time applicant or renewing your insurance plan, understanding how to navigate platforms like HealthCare.gov (the federal exchange) or state-based exchanges will ensure you get the best coverage at the most affordable price. The process can seem overwhelming at first, but with a little guidance and preparation, you'll be able to navigate the system with confidence.

This chapter will take you through the essential steps of applying for subsidies and choosing a health plan through the marketplace. We'll break down how to compare plans, understand coverage options, and meet important deadlines. Additionally, we'll cover some troubleshooting tips to help you resolve common issues that may arise during the application process.

Understanding HealthCare.gov and State-Based Exchanges

The Health Insurance Marketplace is an online platform where individuals and families can shop for, compare, and purchase health insurance. The ACA created these exchanges to help people without employer-sponsored insurance or those who don't qualify for Medicaid or Medicare access affordable health plans.

HealthCare.gov: For states that didn't establish their own marketplace, the federal government operates HealthCare.gov. This platform serves as the central hub for enrollment in states like Texas, Florida, and Georgia.

HealthCare.gov offers both private insurance plans and access to subsidies to make coverage more affordable.

State-Based Marketplaces: Some states have set up their own health insurance exchanges. These state-based platforms often offer additional resources, tailored support, and sometimes expanded options. Examples of states with their own exchanges include California (Covered California), New York (New York State of Health), and Massachusetts (Massachusetts Health Connector).

While the structure and user experience may vary slightly between HealthCare.gov and state-based exchanges, the goal remains the same: to provide a transparent, accessible, and affordable way for individuals to find health insurance.

Key Steps to Apply for Health Insurance Subsidies Through the Marketplace

Applying for health insurance subsidies through the Marketplace can be a straightforward process when you know the steps to take. Here's an overview of the key steps you'll need to follow to apply for coverage:

Step 1: Gather Necessary Information

Before beginning your application, take some time to gather the necessary documentation and information. This will help you move through the process quickly and accurately.

- **Personal Information**: You'll need to provide basic personal details such as your name, address, phone number, and Social Security number.
- **Income Information**: Be prepared to report your estimated household income for the upcoming year. This can include wages, salaries, unemployment benefits, and other sources of income.
- **Household Information**: You'll need to provide information about your household size, including the number of people who will be covered by your insurance plan.
- **Current Health Insurance Information**: If you currently have insurance, you'll need to provide details about your existing plan, such as the plan type, provider, and premiums.

Step 2: Create an Account on HealthCare.gov (or Your State's Marketplace)

To apply for insurance, you need to create an account on HealthCare.gov or your state's marketplace. This involves setting up a username and password, verifying your email, and entering some personal details to set up your profile. Creating an account is free and only takes a few minutes.

Step 3: Fill Out the Application

Once your account is set up, you'll need to complete the application. The marketplace will ask for your income, household size, citizenship status, and other important details. Based on the information you provide, the marketplace will determine if you qualify for subsidies and which health plans are available to you.

- **Income Verification**: You will need to provide proof of your income, which can include recent pay stubs, tax returns, or other financial documents.
- **Eligibility Determination**: After submitting your application, the marketplace will tell you whether you qualify for subsidies such as premium tax credits or cost-sharing reductions.

Step 4: Compare Health Plans

After your eligibility is determined, you'll be able to browse available health insurance plans. The marketplace will show you the plans that meet your needs, and you can compare them based on cost, coverage options, and the providers included in the plan network.

Step 5: Choose a Plan and Enroll

Once you've compared options, choose the plan that best meets your needs and budget. Make sure to review the details, such as monthly premiums, deductibles, co-pays, and out-of-pocket maximums, to ensure the plan is the right fit.

After selecting your plan, you'll need to enroll. During this process, you'll confirm your coverage start date and pay your first premium (if required).

Step 6: Keep Your Application Up-to-Date

If anything changes in your life during the year — such as your income, household size, or employment status — make sure to update your marketplace application. Reporting these changes ensures that your coverage and subsidies remain accurate and up-to-date.

How to Compare Health Plans and Their Costs

Once you've completed the initial steps in the application process, you'll need to compare the available health plans. Understanding the key elements of each plan will help you choose the right one based on your health needs and financial situation.

Key Plan Types

Health insurance plans in the marketplace are categorized into different "metal tiers," which reflect the level of coverage you can expect, as well as the costs of premiums, deductibles, and out-of-pocket expenses. The higher the metal tier, the more the insurance company pays for your medical care, and the lower your out-of-pocket costs will be — but the higher your premiums will be as well.

1. Bronze Plans

- **Best for**: Individuals who are generally healthy and want lower monthly premiums.
- **Coverage**: Bronze plans cover about 60% of your healthcare costs, leaving you to pay the remaining 40%.

- **Premiums**: Lower monthly premiums, but higher deductibles and out-of-pocket costs.
- **Consider**: If you're looking for affordable premiums and don't expect to use a lot of medical care, a Bronze plan may be a good choice.

2. Silver Plans

- **Best for**: People who want a balance between premiums and coverage.
- **Coverage**: Silver plans cover approximately 70% of healthcare costs.
- **Premiums**: Moderate monthly premiums and moderate out-of-pocket costs.
- **Consider**: Silver plans are also the only plans that qualify for Cost-Sharing Reductions (CSRs) if your income is between 100% and 250% of the Federal Poverty Level (FPL).

3. Gold Plans

- **Best for**: Individuals who expect to use healthcare frequently and want higher coverage.
- **Coverage**: Gold plans cover about 80% of your healthcare costs.
- **Premiums**: Higher monthly premiums, but lower out-of-pocket costs.
- **Consider**: If you need frequent medical care, a Gold plan could be ideal for minimizing your out-of-pocket expenses.

4. Platinum Plans

- **Best for**: People who expect to use a lot of healthcare services and want to minimize out-of-pocket costs.
- **Coverage**: Platinum plans cover about 90% of healthcare costs.
- **Premiums**: Highest monthly premiums, but the lowest out-of-pocket costs.
- **Consider**: If you need regular medical care or have chronic conditions, Platinum plans provide the most comprehensive coverage.

Cost Considerations

When comparing plans, consider both your **monthly premium** (the amount you pay every month for coverage) and your **out-of-pocket costs** (including deductibles, copayments, and coinsurance). A lower premium plan might seem more affordable upfront, but it could have higher out-of-pocket costs when you need care. On the other hand, a higher-premium plan might seem more expensive at first but could save you money in the long run if you have frequent healthcare needs.

Out-of-Pocket Maximum: Be sure to look at the plan's out-of-pocket maximum, which is the most you will have to pay for covered services in a year. Once you reach this limit, the insurance will cover 100% of your medical costs for the rest of the year.

Network Considerations: Check whether your preferred doctors and healthcare providers are included in the plan's network. Out-of-network care can be significantly more expensive.

Key Deadlines for Enrollment and Special Enrollment Periods

Knowing when to enroll is crucial to making sure you don't miss out on coverage. There are two main enrollment periods: **Open Enrollment** and **Special Enrollment Periods (SEPs)**.

1. Open Enrollment Period

- The **Open Enrollment Period** is the designated time each year when you can apply for or change your health insurance plan through the marketplace.
- For the 2024 coverage year, the open enrollment period typically starts in November and runs until mid-December, though exact dates may vary each year. During this time, anyone can apply for coverage, regardless of their health status or employment situation.

2. Special Enrollment Periods (SEPs)

You may qualify for a **Special Enrollment Period** if you experience certain life events that affect your health insurance needs. SEPs allow you to apply for or make changes to your insurance plan outside of the Open Enrollment Period. Some examples of life events that trigger an SEP include:

- Getting married or divorced
- Having a baby or adopting a child
- Losing health insurance coverage (e.g., job loss, aging off a parent's plan)

- Moving to a new state or area
- Becoming a U.S. citizen or legal resident

SEPs typically last for 60 days after the qualifying life event. If you miss the SEP window, you will have to wait until the next Open Enrollment Period to apply for or make changes to your plan.

Troubleshooting Common Issues When Navigating the Marketplace

While the marketplace is designed to be user-friendly, you may encounter some issues during the application or enrollment process. Here are some common problems and solutions:

Problem: "I can't log in"

- **Solution**: Double-check your username and password. If you've forgotten your login details, use the "Forgot Username" or "Forgot Password" options to reset them. Ensure you're using the correct website (HealthCare.gov or your state's exchange).

Problem: "I'm not sure if I qualify for subsidies"

- **Solution**: Use the online subsidy calculator on the marketplace website to estimate your eligibility for Premium Tax Credits or Cost-Sharing Reductions. You can also contact the marketplace call center or a local navigator for personalized help.

Problem: "My application is stuck in processing"

- **Solution**: Sometimes, applications can get delayed due to missing information. Make sure all the required fields are filled out, and check your email for any notices from the marketplace asking for additional information.

Problem: "I can't find my doctor in the plan network"

- **Solution**: If your preferred doctor isn't in the plan network, check with the insurance provider directly. You may also want to consider switching to a plan that includes your doctor or finding a new provider within the network.

Conclusion

Navigating the healthcare marketplace may seem intimidating at first, but breaking it down into manageable steps can help simplify the process. By understanding how to apply for subsidies, compare health plans, and meet important deadlines, you'll be able to secure affordable coverage that fits your needs. Be proactive about staying informed, and don't hesitate to reach out for help if you encounter problems along the way. The right plan can significantly improve your health and financial security, so take the time to explore your options and make the best decision for you and your family.

PART 2:
The Changing Landscape – What's New in Subsidies

Chapter 04

COVID-19 and Its Impact on Healthcare Subsidies

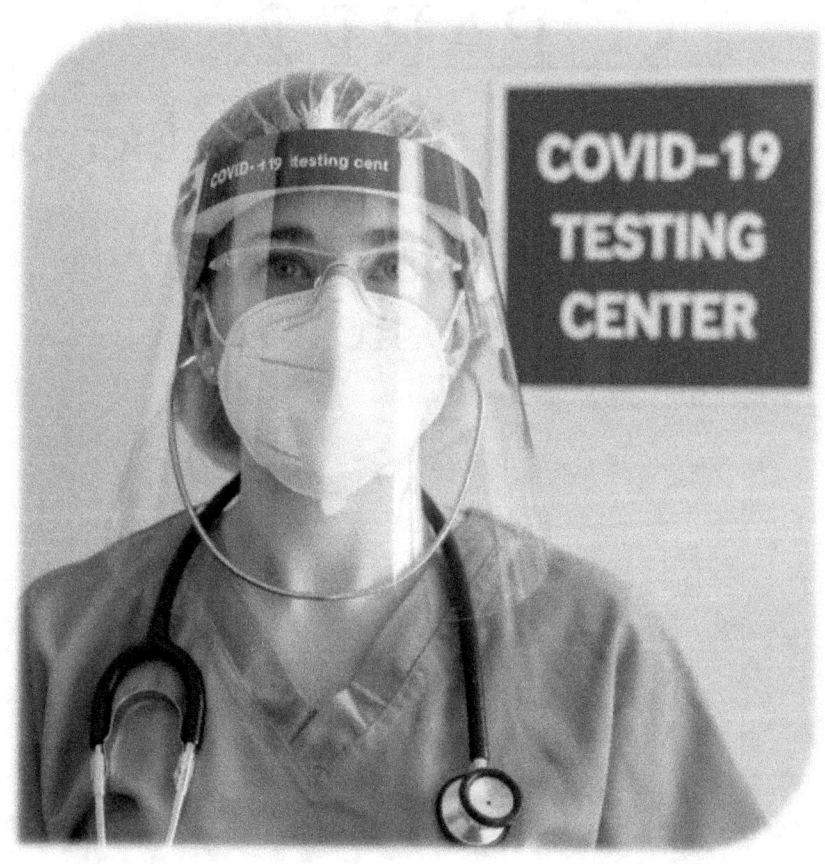

The COVID-19 pandemic reshaped the American healthcare system in profound ways. In addition to highlighting the importance of accessible healthcare, it also underscored the need for affordable insurance options. In response to the public health crisis, the U.S. government enacted several emergency measures to make health coverage more affordable, including significant changes to the subsidies available under the Affordable Care Act (ACA).

One of the most impactful legislative changes came through the **American Rescue Plan (ARP)**, which temporarily expanded ACA subsidies and altered eligibility requirements to ensure that more people could access health insurance during the pandemic. These temporary changes provided immediate relief for millions of Americans, reducing premiums and out-of-pocket costs at a critical time.

As we transition out of the emergency measures introduced during the pandemic, it's important to understand how these changes have impacted healthcare subsidies, how the landscape is shifting, and what you can do to prepare for the expiration of these temporary benefits.

Temporary Changes to Subsidies Under the American Rescue Plan (ARP)

The American Rescue Plan (ARP), passed in March 2021, included provisions that made healthcare coverage through the ACA much more affordable for many Americans. These temporary changes were designed to ease the financial burden of health insurance during the pandemic and to help more people obtain coverage in an environment where job losses and economic instability were widespread.

1. Expanded Eligibility for Premium Tax Credits (PTC)

Before the ARP, Premium Tax Credits (PTC) were available to individuals and families with incomes between 100% and 400% of the Federal Poverty Level (FPL). The ARP temporarily **expanded the income range** for which individuals and families could qualify for these subsidies.

Key Change: The ARP removed the income cap for PTC eligibility, making subsidies available to individuals and families with incomes above 400% of the FPL. This was a significant change, as many people earning more than 400% of the FPL had previously been excluded from subsidies and had to pay full price for their health plans.

Impact: This change allowed many middle- and upper-middle-income families to receive subsidies that dramatically lowered their health insurance premiums. This was particularly helpful for people who had lost employer-sponsored insurance or faced increased financial challenges during the pandemic.

2. Reduction of Premiums for Existing Subsidy Recipients

For those who already qualified for subsidies under the ACA, the ARP made premiums even more affordable.

Key Change: The ARP **reduced the percentage of income** that individuals and families had to pay toward premiums. For example, people with incomes below 150% of the FPL paid as little as $0 per month for a Silver plan. Those with incomes between 150% and 400% of the FPL saw their monthly premiums decrease by hundreds of dollars per month.

Impact: These changes made premiums much more affordable for many people, especially for low- to middle-income families. The ARP also increased the generosity of subsidies, so that many people could get more coverage for less money.

3. Increased Financial Assistance for Cost-Sharing Reductions (CSR)

In addition to expanding Premium Tax Credits, the ARP also provided greater support for **Cost-Sharing Reductions (CSRs)**, which lower out-of-pocket costs for medical services such as copayments, deductibles, and coinsurance.

Key Change: The ARP temporarily enhanced the CSRs available to people with incomes between 100% and 250% of the FPL, reducing out-of-pocket expenses for healthcare services.

Impact: These enhancements made healthcare more affordable for those who had moderate incomes and would normally face higher out-of-pocket costs with a typical health insurance plan. Individuals with lower incomes could access the same level of coverage with fewer financial obstacles when it came to doctor visits, hospital stays, and prescription medications.

Expanding Eligibility for ACA Subsidies (Subsidies for Those Above 400% FPL)

Before the ARP, individuals and families earning more than 400% of the Federal Poverty Level (FPL) were ineligible for Premium Tax Credits and had to pay full price for coverage. This group included many people who did not qualify for other forms of assistance but still struggled to afford premiums in the private insurance market. The ARP introduced a **temporary extension of subsidy eligibility**, which allowed those earning above 400% of the FPL to access Premium Tax Credits.

Key Change: The ARP **eliminated the 400% income cap** for Premium Tax Credits, so individuals and families earning more than this threshold could now qualify for financial assistance, significantly lowering their monthly premiums.

Impact: This change was especially beneficial for middle-class families who were financially squeezed, as well as for those whose income was slightly above the previous subsidy limits but who still struggled with the cost of health insurance premiums.

Example: Under the ARP, a family of four with an income of $110,000 — well above the previous 400% FPL limit — was able to qualify for a substantial Premium Tax Credit. Without this subsidy, they would have had to pay the full premium, which could have been upwards of $1,500 a month or more. With the ARP changes, they could pay far less.

This adjustment allowed for greater affordability in the Marketplace, encouraging more people to sign up for coverage, particularly those who may have been previously discouraged by high premiums.

How the ARP Reduced Premiums and Out-of-Pocket Costs

The ARP's subsidy enhancements helped reduce both premiums and out-of-pocket costs for many individuals and families. Here's a look at how these changes made healthcare more affordable:

1. Lower Monthly Premiums

- **Enhanced Subsidies**: The ARP increased the amount of financial assistance available to low- and middle-income families, which directly reduced their monthly premiums.
- **Zero Premium Plans**: Some individuals earning up to 150% of the FPL qualified for **$0 premium plans** in the Marketplace, meaning they could access a Silver-level plan with no monthly cost.
- **Premium Reductions**: For those with incomes between 150% and 400% of the FPL, the ARP

lowered premiums by a significant percentage, allowing them to pay far less each month.

2. Reduced Out-of-Pocket Costs

In addition to lowering premiums, the ARP enhanced Cost-Sharing Reductions (CSRs), making healthcare more affordable for people when they actually seek care.

- **Lower Deductibles and Copayments**: CSRs helped to reduce deductibles, copayments, and coinsurance, meaning that people with lower incomes could afford to seek medical care when needed without facing high upfront costs.
- **More Affordable Prescription Drugs**: Reduced copays and coinsurance for prescriptions, especially for those in lower income brackets, helped ease the burden of out-of-pocket costs for medications.

3. Expanded Coverage for More People

The reduction in both premiums and out-of-pocket costs helped more individuals and families afford health insurance coverage. The ability to access low- or no-cost plans through the Marketplace made it easier for previously uninsured Americans to get the coverage they needed.

The Transition Back to Pre-ARP Subsidy Rules

While the ARP made healthcare more affordable for many Americans, these temporary measures are set to expire. As we transition back to the pre-ARP subsidy rules, it's essential to understand what changes will occur and how they might impact you.

1. Reverting to the 400% FPL Income Cap

One of the most significant changes is the reversion to the **400% Federal Poverty Level (FPL) income cap** for eligibility for Premium Tax Credits. If your income exceeds 400% of the FPL, you will no longer qualify for subsidies and will have to pay the full premium amount.

2. Premium Increases for Many People

Without the enhanced subsidies provided by the ARP, many individuals and families will see a rise in their monthly premiums. For those who earned more than 400% of the FPL, this may result in significant premium increases as they no longer qualify for subsidies.

3. Increased Out-of-Pocket Costs

Cost-sharing reductions will also revert to their pre-ARP levels, meaning that those who previously enjoyed lower copayments and deductibles may find that their out-of-pocket costs are higher again.

Key Takeaways: What Happens When Emergency Provisions End

As we transition out of the emergency provisions, it's important to be proactive and understand the implications of these changes. Here are the key takeaways:

- **Increased Premiums**: Many individuals and families will experience a rise in their monthly premiums as the temporary ARP subsidies expire.
- **Loss of Subsidies for High-Income Earners**: Those who earn more than 400% of the FPL will once again be ineligible for Premium Tax Credits, leading to full-price premiums.
- **Higher Out-of-Pocket Costs**: Cost-sharing reductions will return to their previous levels, meaning higher copays, deductibles, and coinsurance for many people.
- **More Expensive Coverage**: Without the ARP enhancements, coverage could become unaffordable for some individuals and families who were previously benefiting from the subsidies.

Action Steps to Take Before and After the Expiration of Temporary Benefits

Here are some actionable steps to take before and after the expiration of the temporary ARP benefits:

Before the Expiration:

- **Review Your Current Plan**: Take the time to assess your current plan's premium, coverage, and out-of-pocket costs. Determine if you will be able to afford the plan once the ARP subsidies expire.

➢ **Update Your Marketplace Application**: If your income has changed or you've had a life event (e.g., marriage, childbirth), update your application to reflect these changes. You may still qualify for some level of subsidy.

➢ **Consider Switching Plans**: Explore whether there are more affordable plans available to you as the temporary subsidies expire. You may need to shift to a different plan to keep your healthcare costs manageable.

After the Expiration:

➢ **Prepare for Increased Costs**: Set aside extra funds to cover potential increases in premiums and out-of-pocket costs.
➢ **Look for Other Assistance**: If you're no longer eligible for subsidies, consider other forms of assistance such as Medicaid or employer-based coverage if applicable.
➢ **Stay Informed**: Keep an eye on future legislative changes. Healthcare policy is constantly evolving, and new opportunities for assistance may become available.

Conclusion

The COVID-19 pandemic and the American Rescue Plan brought significant changes to the landscape of healthcare subsidies, making health insurance more affordable for millions of Americans. However, as temporary emergency measures end, it's important to prepare for the transition back to pre-ARP subsidy rules. By understanding the changes that have occurred and taking action before the benefits expire, you can make informed decisions about your healthcare and ensure that you and your family remain covered.

Chapter 05

The Inflation Reduction Act and Its Impact on ACA Subsidies

The **Inflation Reduction Act (IRA)**, passed in August 2022, is one of the most significant pieces of legislation in recent U.S. history, affecting a broad range of sectors from climate change and energy to healthcare. For millions of Americans who rely on health insurance subsidies, the IRA has brought vital changes that extend and enhance the subsidies offered through the Affordable Care Act (ACA). This chapter will provide a comprehensive overview of how the IRA impacts ACA subsidies, who benefits, and what the future holds once these provisions expire.

Overview of the Inflation Reduction Act (IRA) and Its Key Healthcare Provisions

The Inflation Reduction Act (IRA) is a sweeping law designed to lower prescription drug prices, reduce healthcare costs, and combat inflation. While its focus is on many sectors of the economy, its provisions related to healthcare subsidies under the ACA are particularly significant. One of the key healthcare provisions of the IRA is the **extension of enhanced subsidies for health insurance purchased through the ACA's health insurance marketplaces**.

Enhanced Premium Tax Credits: Prior to the IRA, the **American Rescue Plan (ARP)** temporarily enhanced subsidies to make health insurance more affordable for millions of Americans. The IRA extended these enhanced subsidies, providing financial relief to individuals and families who may have struggled to afford ACA coverage before these enhancements were made.

Prescription Drug Price Relief: In addition to the subsidies for marketplace coverage, the IRA also introduced provisions to lower prescription drug prices, including price caps on certain medications and negotiated drug prices for Medicare recipients. These provisions, though not directly related to ACA subsidies, contribute to the broader goal of reducing overall healthcare costs for Americans.

How the IRA Extended Enhanced Subsidies Through 2025

One of the most important aspects of the IRA for ACA subsidy recipients is the **extension of the enhanced subsidies** originally implemented by the American Rescue Plan (ARP). These subsidies were a temporary measure designed to provide immediate relief during the COVID-19 pandemic, but under the IRA, they were extended through **2025**.

Key Provisions of the IRA Subsidy Extension

Extended Duration: The IRA provides a critical extension of the **temporary enhanced subsidies** for **three more years**, through 2025. This means that eligible individuals and families will continue to receive significantly lower premiums and out-of-pocket costs compared to what they would have paid under the original ACA subsidy rules, which were in place before the ARP enhancements.

Continued Eligibility for Middle-Class Families: The IRA extends eligibility for Premium Tax Credits (PTCs) to families and individuals earning more than 400% of the Federal Poverty Level (FPL), which was a major benefit of the ARP. The IRA ensures that people who were previously excluded from receiving subsidies due to their higher incomes will still benefit from enhanced financial assistance for the next few years.

Increased Financial Assistance: The law provides more generous subsidies, lowering premium costs for millions of Americans. For example, many people who were paying high premiums will find that they can continue to afford a health plan with lower premiums and more generous cost-sharing.

Expanding Eligibility to a Larger Pool of Americans

One of the most notable features of the IRA's impact on ACA subsidies is the expansion of eligibility to a **larger pool of Americans**, particularly those who were previously excluded due to their higher incomes.

1. Extending Subsidies Beyond 400% of the Federal Poverty Level (FPL)

Prior to the ARP, people with incomes above **400% of the FPL** were not eligible for Premium Tax Credits (PTCs). With the IRA's extension of the enhanced subsidies, **those with incomes above 400% FPL** can now receive assistance. This is a significant benefit for **middle-income families** who typically earn too much to qualify for subsidies but still struggle to afford premiums on the open market.

> **Example**: A family of four with an income of $110,000 per year, which is approximately 400% of the FPL, would have been ineligible for ACA subsidies before the ARP. Now, under the IRA, that family may be eligible for a substantial Premium Tax Credit, lowering their monthly premium costs.

2. Increased Coverage for Low-Income Americans

The IRA also continues to provide **financial relief for low-income Americans** by extending subsidies that ensure individuals earning **up to 150% of the FPL** may qualify for $0 premiums for coverage. For individuals earning **between 150% and 250% FPL**, the IRA continues to provide enhanced subsidies, which lower premiums and reduce cost-sharing.

3. Expanded Access for Middle-Class Families

Middle-class families who earned above 400% of the FPL will continue to benefit from expanded eligibility. This is especially important because **before the IRA, families earning above 400% of the FPL were forced to purchase insurance at full price**, which was often unaffordable.

> **Example**: A **single individual earning $70,000 per year** (just over 400% of FPL) would likely pay a high monthly premium for an ACA plan without subsidies. Under the IRA, this individual would continue to qualify for premium assistance, reducing monthly costs and making health insurance more accessible.

The Impact on Middle-Income Earners Who Previously Didn't Qualify

The IRA has been particularly impactful for **middle-income earners** who previously didn't qualify for subsidies. Prior to the enhanced subsidies, many middle-class individuals and families faced high premiums and out-of-pocket costs when purchasing coverage through the ACA marketplace. For families earning more than 400% of the FPL, the full price of premiums was often prohibitively expensive, leading many to forgo health insurance altogether or face financial strain in purchasing a plan.

How the IRA Benefits Middle-Income Earners

Lower Monthly Premiums: With the IRA's extension of the enhanced subsidies, **middle-income families** will pay significantly lower premiums than they would have under the original ACA rules. These families will also have access to a wider range of affordable plans, giving them more flexibility and choice when selecting coverage.

Wider Access to Silver, Gold, and Platinum Plans: Many middle-income families who previously found themselves in the **Bronze plan category** due to high premiums may now be able to afford **Silver**, **Gold**, or even **Platinum** plans. These plans offer better coverage, lower deductibles, and more comprehensive benefits, making them more attractive to those who can now afford them.

Example: A **family of four earning $85,000 a year** would have previously faced a significant financial burden in paying full premiums for health insurance. Under the IRA's provisions, they can qualify for subsidies that reduce their premiums and potentially lower their out-of-pocket costs, giving them access to higher-tier plans at a more affordable price.

How to Maximize IRA-Enhanced Subsidies

If you qualify for enhanced subsidies under the IRA, it's important to understand how to maximize the financial assistance available to you. By carefully navigating the health insurance marketplace and making informed decisions, you can lower your monthly premiums, reduce out-of-pocket costs, and choose the health plan that best meets your needs.

1. Shop Around During Open Enrollment

To make sure you're getting the most affordable coverage, take the time to shop around during the **Open Enrollment Period**. Even if you've had the same plan for years, it's important to compare new plans every year to ensure you're getting the best deal. Plans may change from year to year, and new providers may enter the marketplace.

> **Action Step**: Compare plans not only based on premiums but also on coverage options, out-of-pocket costs (like deductibles and copayments), and whether your preferred healthcare providers are included in the plan's network.

2. Report Changes in Income or Family Size

Since your Premium Tax Credit is based on your household's income and size, it's essential to **update your application** if your income or family size changes. Reporting these changes will help ensure you're receiving the correct subsidy amount.

> **Action Step**: If you get a raise, lose a job, have a baby, or experience any other major life change, make sure to update your information on the marketplace as soon as possible.

3. Consider the Silver Plan for Cost-Sharing Reductions

If you qualify for Cost-Sharing Reductions (CSRs), the **Silver plan** is often the best option to maximize your savings. Silver plans are the only ones that provide CSR benefits, which help lower your out-of-pocket costs when you need care.

➢ **Action Step**: If you qualify for CSRs, it's important to choose a **Silver plan** rather than a Bronze or Gold plan, as Silver plans provide the best combination of premium affordability and out-of-pocket cost reductions.

Future Considerations: What Happens After 2025?

While the IRA extends enhanced subsidies through 2025, there is still uncertainty about what will happen once these provisions expire. The future of healthcare subsidies beyond 2025 largely depends on political factors, including whether Congress decides to extend these provisions or whether new legislation is introduced.

Potential Scenarios After 2025

Extension of Subsidies: Given the popularity of enhanced subsidies and the positive impact they've had on millions of Americans, there may be a push to **extend the enhanced subsidies beyond 2025**. Public support for more affordable healthcare is strong, and many political leaders may prioritize making these changes permanent.

Reversion to Pre-ARP Subsidies: If no extension occurs, we could see a **return to pre-ARP subsidy rules**. This would likely mean higher premiums and a reduction in financial assistance, particularly for those above 400% of the FPL.

What You Can Do to Prepare

- **Stay Informed**: Keep an eye on legislative updates regarding healthcare policy and ACA subsidies. Being informed about changes will help you plan ahead and avoid surprises when 2025 rolls around.
- **Consider Alternative Coverage Options**: If subsidies are reduced or eliminated after 2025, explore other options, such as **Medicaid**, **Medicare** (if you're eligible), or employer-based insurance.
- **Plan for Potential Cost Increases**: Start budgeting for the possibility of higher premiums and out-of-pocket costs in the future, particularly if the enhanced subsidies are not extended.

Conclusion

The Inflation Reduction Act has had a profound impact on healthcare subsidies, extending enhanced financial assistance through 2025 and making health insurance more affordable for millions of Americans. This extension benefits a broader range of people, particularly middle-income families who were previously ineligible for subsidies. By understanding how to navigate the enhanced subsidies, you can maximize your financial assistance, lower your premiums, and ensure you have access to the health coverage you need. However, it's important to stay informed about future policy changes, as the expiration of these provisions could significantly impact your healthcare costs.

Chapter 06
State-Specific Changes to Healthcare Subsidies

While the **Affordable Care Act (ACA)** established a national framework for healthcare coverage and subsidies, individual states have significant power to modify and enhance these provisions to meet the specific needs of their populations. States can make decisions regarding the expansion of Medicaid, the establishment of state-based health insurance exchanges, and the implementation of innovative premium assistance programs. This chapter will explore the state-specific changes to healthcare subsidies, highlight examples of states with unique subsidy programs, and offer key actions steps for individuals in states with significant ACA reforms.

How States Can Modify Medicaid and ACA Provisions

One of the most important aspects of the ACA was the expansion of Medicaid eligibility to cover more low-income Americans. However, not all states chose to adopt this expansion, leaving millions without access to affordable healthcare.

Medicaid Expansion:

The ACA initially offered federal funds to states to expand Medicaid to individuals earning up to 138% of the **Federal Poverty Level (FPL)**. As of 2023, **40 states and the District of Columbia** have opted to expand Medicaid, while 12 states have not. These states have their own unique challenges, as individuals who fall into the **"coverage gap"** (earning too much to qualify for Medicaid, but too little to qualify for ACA subsidies) may be left without access to affordable healthcare.

> **Key Impact**: States that have expanded Medicaid have significantly reduced the uninsured rate in their populations, providing health insurance to millions of people who would otherwise be ineligible for coverage. On the other hand, individuals in non-expansion states remain in a position where they may have to turn to private insurance, which is often unaffordable.

State-Specific Medicaid Expansion Decisions:

Some states have chosen to implement Medicaid expansion with adjustments to fit local needs. For example:

> **Arkansas** and **Indiana** expanded Medicaid through **Alternative Benefit Plans**, giving them more flexibility in offering services and reducing costs for the state.
> **Montana** implemented Medicaid expansion under a **waiver program**, which included more stringent work requirements and premium contributions from certain beneficiaries.

This flexibility in how Medicaid is expanded means that, depending on where you live, the specific eligibility criteria, coverage, and costs can vary.

Action Steps for Medicaid Expansion States:

- ➤ **If your state has expanded Medicaid**: Take advantage of the expanded coverage. Apply through your state's Medicaid program to ensure you are receiving the benefits you are eligible for, particularly if your income is at or below 138% of the FPL.
- ➤ **If your state has not expanded Medicaid**: Investigate whether there are state-run programs or eligibility pathways that could provide coverage, such as state-funded healthcare programs or access to the ACA marketplace subsidies.

State-Specific Health Insurance Exchanges: What Changes Should You Expect?

In addition to Medicaid expansion, states have the authority to create their own **state-based health insurance exchanges** (also known as **marketplaces**), instead of using the federal marketplace, HealthCare.gov. Having a state-run marketplace allows states to tailor their offerings, set their own policies, and better address local healthcare needs.

State-based Marketplaces vs. HealthCare.gov:

While all states can use HealthCare.gov to enroll in ACA health plans, some states have opted to set up their own exchanges. As of 2023, **17 states and the District of Columbia** operate their own exchanges, while the remaining states rely on the federal marketplace.

- ➤ **Advantages of State-Based Marketplaces**:

> **Local Support**: State exchanges can provide more localized customer support and resources, making it easier for residents to navigate the enrollment process and understand local health plans.
> **Customized Plans**: States can offer health plans that are better suited to local needs, including plans with a more regionally appropriate set of benefits.
> **State-Level Premium Assistance**: Some states provide additional financial assistance for premiums or out-of-pocket costs, helping residents access even more affordable plans.

Examples of States with State-Based Marketplaces:

California: The **Covered California** marketplace is one of the most well-established state exchanges. It offers an **additional state subsidy** to lower-income residents and has a reputation for user-friendly enrollment. California also offers premium assistance to households making more than 400% of the FPL, an initiative that further helps middle-class families.

New York: **New York State of Health**, the state marketplace, also offers a robust selection of health plans, and residents can qualify for enhanced subsidies based on their income. New York has further embraced ACA provisions by enhancing Medicaid and offering assistance with premiums for middle-income households.

Massachusetts: **The Massachusetts Health Connector** provides coverage options with subsidies and premium assistance. The state also runs a

premium assistance program to help residents who purchase insurance through the marketplace, which can be especially helpful for middle-income earners who are close to the eligibility threshold for ACA subsidies.

How to Navigate State-Specific Marketplaces:

- **Research Your State's Marketplace**: Visit your state's health insurance exchange website to learn more about available plans, subsidies, and additional assistance programs.
- **Use Local Resources**: Take advantage of local resources, such as community outreach programs, to guide you through the enrollment process and help you understand your options.

Examples of States with Innovative Subsidy Programs

Some states have implemented **innovative subsidy programs** that go beyond what is offered through the federal ACA marketplace. These programs aim to fill in the gaps in healthcare coverage and make it more affordable for residents, especially in areas where federal subsidies may not go far enough.

California: Additional State-Specific Subsidies

- California has adopted additional subsidies through **California's State-Based Premium Assistance Program** for individuals earning between **400% and 600% of the FPL**. This program provides subsidies to families who would not otherwise qualify for ACA subsidies, making coverage more affordable for the middle class. The state also uses **reinsurance** programs, which help reduce premiums by covering some of the most expensive claims.

New York: Premium Assistance for the Middle Class

> In addition to the ACA subsidies, **New York State of Health** offers **premium assistance programs** for people with incomes up to **500% of the FPL**, helping people in the upper-middle class manage healthcare costs. This assistance allows middle-income individuals and families to afford higher-tier plans (Gold, Platinum) that offer more comprehensive coverage.

Oregon: The Oregon Reinsurance Program

> **Oregon** has implemented the **Oregon Reinsurance Program**, which helps lower premiums by providing funding to insurers to help cover the cost of high-risk claims. This program has been especially beneficial for people who purchase individual plans through the marketplace, as it results in significantly lower premiums.

Understanding State-Based Premium Assistance Programs

In addition to the federal subsidies available through the ACA marketplace, some states have developed **state-based premium assistance programs**. These programs are designed to reduce the financial burden of insurance for residents who may not qualify for Medicaid but still need help affording coverage.

How State-Based Premium Assistance Works:

- **Eligibility**: Each state will have its own eligibility requirements for premium assistance, typically based on income. In some states, assistance may extend to individuals with incomes just above the federal eligibility threshold, helping to close the "subsidy gap."
- **Enhanced Subsidies**: Some states use state funds to offer additional subsidies on top of federal subsidies, further reducing the cost of premiums or offering **cost-sharing reductions** for eligible enrollees.
- **Example**: **California** offers a sliding-scale subsidy for households with incomes up to **600% of the FPL**, meaning that families with higher incomes can still receive significant financial assistance, even if they are not eligible for federal subsidies.

Action Steps for Benefiting from State-Based Premium Assistance:

- **Check for State-Specific Programs**: Research if your state has a premium assistance program. This

may include visiting your state's marketplace website or consulting with a local health advisor.
- **Apply for Additional Subsidies**: If you qualify for additional state subsidies, make sure to apply through your state's marketplace. Ensure that all required documents, such as income verification and household size, are up-to-date.

Adjusting to State-Level Policy Shifts and Timelines

Changes to ACA and Medicaid policies can vary greatly from state to state. States may adjust their health insurance offerings and deadlines based on changes in local legislation or new federal mandates. It is important to be aware of these shifts and how they might affect your healthcare coverage.

1. Understanding Timelines for Open Enrollment and Special Enrollment:

Each state's **open enrollment period** and **special enrollment periods (SEPs)** can vary. While most states follow the federal timeline for ACA open enrollment, some states with state-based marketplaces may have different deadlines.

- **Action Step**: Mark important enrollment dates for your state on your calendar. This ensures you won't miss the opportunity to apply for or renew your coverage.

2. Tracking Legislative Changes:

State legislatures can pass laws that affect healthcare access and subsidies, such as changes to Medicaid eligibility or the introduction of new state-funded assistance programs. Keeping track of these changes is essential to making sure you're maximizing your eligibility.

➤ **Action Step**: Stay informed about **state-level healthcare legislation** by following updates from your state's health department or marketplace. Subscribe to newsletters or notifications from local healthcare advocacy groups that track changes.

Key Action Steps for Those in States with Major ACA Reforms

If you live in a state with **significant ACA reforms**, such as **California, New York,** or **Massachusetts**, you have the opportunity to access additional subsidies or more generous health plans. To take full advantage of state-specific reforms:

1. **Review Your Eligibility**: Ensure that your income and household size meet the requirements for additional state-based subsidies or premium assistance programs.
2. **Explore All Available Health Plans**: Take advantage of the variety of health plans offered through your state's exchange. Look beyond premiums and consider other factors, like coverage and out-of-pocket costs, to make the best choice.

3. **Monitor Legislative Changes**: Stay updated on any new laws or programs that could affect your healthcare costs or coverage options.

Conclusion

State-specific changes to healthcare subsidies and Medicaid provisions are crucial in shaping the healthcare landscape for millions of Americans. By understanding the nuances of your state's health insurance marketplace, Medicaid expansion decisions, and innovative subsidy programs, you can make informed choices about your healthcare coverage. Whether you're in a state that has implemented expanded Medicaid or one with its own health insurance exchange, being proactive and staying informed will help you navigate the evolving healthcare subsidy landscape with confidence.

Part 3: Maximizing Your Healthcare Benefits

Chapter 07
Maximizing Your Healthcare Benefits

One of the most important steps in navigating the Affordable Care Act (ACA) and maximizing your healthcare benefits is determining your eligibility for subsidies. Subsidies can significantly reduce the cost of health insurance premiums, making coverage more affordable for individuals and families. In this chapter, we'll explore how to evaluate your eligibility based on household income and size, how to use tools like the Marketplace calculator to estimate your subsidy, and special considerations for self-employed individuals and small business owners. Additionally, we will discuss how life changes can affect your eligibility and what action steps to take to ensure you're receiving the maximum subsidy you're entitled to.

How to Determine if You're Eligible for Subsidies Based on Household Income and Size

The eligibility for **Premium Tax Credits (PTCs)** and **Cost-Sharing Reductions (CSRs)** depends on several factors, but the two most critical criteria are your **household income** and **household size**. Subsidies are designed to make healthcare more affordable for those who need it the most, so understanding how these two factors influence your eligibility is essential.

1. Household Income:

To determine if you qualify for subsidies, the first step is to compare your **household income** to the **Federal Poverty Level (FPL)**. The ACA uses a sliding scale, which means the lower your income, the higher your subsidy will be. In 2023, for example, the FPL is approximately:

> $14,580 for a single person.
> $30,000 for a family of four.

Key Eligibility Thresholds:

> **Premium Tax Credits (PTC)**: You may qualify for PTC if your income is between **100% and 400% of the FPL**. This means individuals and families with incomes between these levels can receive financial assistance to lower their monthly premiums.
> **Cost-Sharing Reductions (CSR)**: If your income is between **100% and 250% of the FPL**, you may qualify for CSRs, which help reduce your out-of-pocket costs (such as deductibles, co-pays, and coinsurance) in addition to lowering your premiums.

2. Household Size:

Your **household size** includes everyone who is considered part of your tax family (dependents, children, and anyone who is legally obligated to be included in your tax return). The **larger your household**, the higher the FPL threshold will be for eligibility. This is why it's important to carefully calculate your household size when applying for subsidies.

> **Example**: A single individual with an income of **$50,000** may not qualify for subsidies (since it's above 400% FPL), but a **family of four with the**

same income might qualify for some subsidy assistance.

Income vs. FPL:

Understanding where you fall within the FPL guidelines is crucial. If your income is **just above** the cutoff for subsidies (for example, you earn 401% of the FPL), you may be left without assistance, leading to higher premiums. On the other hand, if your income is **just below** the subsidy threshold, you might qualify for **significant savings** on your health coverage.

The Importance of Household Income Verification

One of the most critical steps when applying for subsidies is **accurately reporting your household income**. This includes all sources of income, such as:

- **Wages or salary**
- **Self-employment income**
- **Unemployment benefits**
- **Investment income**
- **Social Security, pension, or disability income**

Income Verification Process:

The Health Insurance Marketplace requires you to provide documentation to verify your income, which might include:

- **Pay stubs**
- **Tax returns (Form 1040)**
- **W-2 forms**
- **Bank statements or other financial records**

Accurate income verification is essential to avoid future problems with subsidy reconciliation. If you receive too much subsidy based on inaccurate income reporting, you may be required to repay the excess amount when filing your taxes. On the other hand, if you underreport your income, you may miss out on subsidies that you are eligible for.

What Happens if Your Income Changes During the Year?

If your income changes during the year (e.g., a pay raise, job loss, or change in working hours), it's critical to report this change to the Marketplace as soon as possible. Failure to update your income information can lead to either **overpayment** or **underpayment** of your subsidies.

Using the Marketplace Calculator to Estimate Subsidies

The **Marketplace subsidy calculator** is an incredibly useful tool that can help you estimate your eligibility for subsidies and how much assistance you may receive. This tool can give you a rough idea of what your monthly premium could be, depending on your household income, size, and where you live.

How the Calculator Works:

- **Enter your household size**: The calculator will ask for your household members, including any dependents.
- **Enter your household income**: This should be your modified adjusted gross income (MAGI), which includes all income sources.
- **Select your state**: Subsidies can vary based on your state of residence, so knowing your location will help provide a more accurate estimate.
- **Estimate your premiums**: The calculator will provide an estimated monthly premium for each of the **metal-tier plans** (Bronze, Silver, Gold, and Platinum) available to you. It will also show you the amount of financial assistance you may receive.

How to Use the Results:

- **Compare plans**: Once you have your subsidy estimate, you can compare plans to see which one fits your healthcare needs and budget.
- **Consider cost-sharing**: If you qualify for **Cost-Sharing Reductions**, the calculator will help you identify which plan will lower your out-of-pocket costs.
- **Make adjustments as needed**: If you find that you do not qualify for subsidies or that the premium is still too high, you may consider adjusting your household's income (for example, by including income from a spouse) or exploring other options such as Medicaid or employer-sponsored plans.

Special Considerations for Self-Employed Individuals and Small Business Owners

Self-employed individuals and small business owners face unique challenges when determining their eligibility for ACA subsidies. Since they don't have access to employer-sponsored health insurance, they must rely on the Health Insurance Marketplace to secure coverage. Additionally, their income is often more variable and difficult to estimate.

1. How to Calculate Income for Subsidy Eligibility:

Self-employed individuals and small business owners can deduct certain business expenses when calculating their Modified Adjusted Gross Income (MAGI), which may lower their total income and increase their chances of qualifying for subsidies. These deductions could include:

- **Business operating expenses** (e.g., office supplies, marketing, utilities)
- **Self-employed health insurance premiums** (if you pay for your own health coverage)
- **Retirement contributions** (e.g., IRA or 401(k) contributions)

2. Using Tax Returns to Estimate Income:

When applying for subsidies, it's important to use **previous year's tax returns** as a reference for estimating your income. If your income fluctuates or varies greatly throughout the year, it's advisable to project an **annual income estimate** based on your current situation, but with adjustments for any major income changes expected during the year.

3. Special Enrollment Periods (SEPs):

Small business owners or self-employed individuals may qualify for **Special Enrollment Periods** (SEPs) if they lose other health coverage (for example, if their spouse's employer-sponsored coverage is lost). In these cases, they can apply for ACA coverage even outside of the regular Open Enrollment Period.

4. Managing Irregular Income:

If your income is irregular, consider setting aside extra funds for months where income may be lower. Additionally, you can **update your Marketplace application** as often as needed if your income or business revenue changes during the year.

Impact of Life Changes on Subsidy Eligibility (Marriage, Job Change, etc.)

Changes in your life circumstances can dramatically affect your eligibility for subsidies. Life events such as **marriage**, **job changes**, **birth of a child**, or **moving to a new state** can all impact your income and household size, thereby affecting the subsidies available to you.

Key Life Events that Affect Subsidy Eligibility:

Marriage: If you get married, you'll need to update your application to include your spouse's income, which could change your eligibility for subsidies. If your combined household income increases significantly, you may no longer qualify for subsidies.

Job Loss or Job Change: Losing your job or changing employers can significantly affect your income and health insurance coverage. If you lose employer-sponsored coverage, you may qualify for a Special Enrollment Period (SEP) and can apply for a Marketplace plan with subsidies.

Birth or Adoption of a Child: A birth or adoption can increase your household size, which may increase your subsidy eligibility, particularly if you have dependents under 18 years of age.

Change in Residency: Moving to a new state may affect the state-based marketplace you use, the available plans, and your eligibility for subsidies. Be sure to update your application with your new address as soon as possible to ensure continuity of coverage and accurate subsidy determination.

Action Steps to Take After a Life Change:

1. **Report Changes Promptly**: As soon as a life change occurs, visit the Marketplace to update your application with new income, household size, or residency information.
2. **Review Your Eligibility**: After reporting the change, review your eligibility for subsidies. If

you're now eligible for more assistance, make sure to apply for the increased subsidy. Conversely, if your eligibility has decreased, adjust your budget accordingly.

Conclusion

Evaluating your eligibility for ACA subsidies is an essential step toward securing affordable healthcare coverage. By understanding the importance of household income, family size, and reporting life changes promptly, you can maximize your subsidy benefits and make informed decisions about your healthcare options. For self-employed individuals and small business owners, special considerations like irregular income and tax deductions are crucial for determining your eligibility. With these actionable steps, you can ensure that you're receiving the full benefits available to you, giving you the security and peace of mind that comes with quality health coverage.

Chapter 08

Choosing the Right Health Insurance Plan for You

Choosing the right health insurance plan can be a daunting task, especially when you're balancing the need for affordable premiums with the desire for comprehensive coverage. Fortunately, the **Affordable Care Act (ACA)** and the accompanying subsidies can make this process more manageable by lowering your premium costs and improving access to a variety of plans. This chapter will guide you through the key factors to consider when selecting a health insurance plan, how to evaluate plans based on your specific needs, and how to maximize the value of your subsidy to make the best choice for you and your family.

How to Evaluate Health Plans Based on Your Needs (Doctor Access, Prescription Coverage)

The first step in choosing the right health insurance plan is to consider your **specific healthcare needs**. Everyone has different health requirements, and your health insurance plan should reflect that. Below are the key elements to consider:

1. Access to Your Doctors and Specialists

- **In-Network vs. Out-of-Network**: Health insurance plans typically have **provider networks**, which are groups of doctors, hospitals, and other healthcare providers that have agreed to provide services at negotiated rates. Choosing a plan that includes your preferred healthcare providers in-network can significantly lower your costs.

✓ **Action Step**: Check the plan's network list to ensure your primary care doctor, specialists, and hospitals are covered. Many insurance providers offer online tools where you can search for in-network providers.

➢ **Referral Requirements**: Some plans, especially **Health Maintenance Organizations (HMOs)**, may require you to get a referral from a primary care doctor before seeing a specialist, while others (such as **Preferred Provider Organizations (PPOs)**) allow you to see specialists without a referral.

✓ **Action Step**: If seeing a specialist without a referral is important to you, consider choosing a PPO or another plan type that offers this flexibility.

2. Prescription Drug Coverage

➢ **Formulary**: Health insurance plans also have a **formulary**, which is a list of prescription drugs that are covered under the plan. Make sure that your regular prescriptions are included in the formulary, and if you have specific medications, check for any restrictions.

✓ **Action Step**: Before selecting a plan, check its formulary for your medications and compare the cost-sharing arrangements. Some plans may have lower co-pays for generic drugs or offer higher-tier coverage for specialized medications.

➢ **Prescription Tiering**: Many plans group medications into tiers based on cost (e.g., Tier 1 for generics, Tier 2 for preferred brand names, and Tier 3 for non-preferred drugs). Make sure your medications fall into the lower-cost tiers if possible.

✓ **Action Step**: Consider the cost-sharing for prescription medications in your plan choices. For high-cost medications, make sure the plan provides adequate coverage and affordable co-pays or coinsurance.

3. Preventive Care and Wellness Services

➢ **Preventive Care Coverage**: All ACA-compliant plans are required to cover a range of **preventive services** without charging a co-pay or deductible, such as vaccinations, screenings, and counseling. Check that your chosen plan includes preventive care services that are important to you.

✓ **Action Step**: Review the preventive services offered by the plan. If you have specific health concerns or risk factors (e.g., cancer screenings, heart disease), ensure these are covered.

Comparing Plans in Terms of Premiums, Deductibles, and Out-of-Pocket Maximums

Once you've narrowed down your options based on your healthcare needs, it's time to compare plans on financial terms. These factors play a huge role in how much you will pay for your insurance each month and when you need medical care.

1. Monthly Premiums

➤ The **premium** is the amount you pay every month to keep your health insurance coverage active. Subsidies can lower the amount you pay for premiums, which makes a significant difference in your overall healthcare costs.

✓ **Action Step**: Use the subsidy calculator on the Health Insurance Marketplace to see how much your premium will be after subsidies. Ensure that the premium fits within your budget, but don't base your decision on premiums alone.

2. Deductibles

➤ The **deductible** is the amount you must pay for healthcare services before your insurance plan starts to pay. Generally, higher deductible plans have lower premiums, but you'll pay more upfront before your insurance kicks in.

✓ **Action Step**: If you expect to have significant medical expenses (e.g., a chronic condition), a plan with a **lower deductible** may be more cost-effective in the long run, even if it means paying a higher premium.

3. Out-of-Pocket Maximums

- ➤ The **out-of-pocket maximum** is the most you'll have to pay for covered services in a year. Once you reach this amount, the plan will pay 100% of your covered services for the remainder of the year. This is an important factor to consider if you anticipate needing significant medical care.

- ✓ **Action Step**: Compare out-of-pocket maximums between plans. If you expect high medical costs, a plan with a **lower out-of-pocket maximum** might be a better choice, as it limits how much you'll have to spend on healthcare each year.

4. Cost-Sharing Features

- ➤ **Co-pays** and **coinsurance** are additional costs you'll need to pay when you receive services, such as doctor visits, prescriptions, or emergency room visits. Plans with lower co-pays and coinsurance are generally more expensive upfront, but can be beneficial for people who need frequent care.

- ✓ **Action Step**: Look at the co-pays for doctor visits, emergency care, and prescriptions. If you plan to visit the doctor regularly or take several prescriptions, a plan with lower co-pays can save you money over time.

The Role of Subsidies in Making Higher-Tier Plans More Affordable

One of the key advantages of ACA health plans is that subsidies can help make **higher-tier plans** (Gold and

Platinum plans) more affordable, even if you don't qualify for full Medicaid coverage.

Understanding Metal Tiers:

- **Bronze**: The least expensive option, but with the highest out-of-pocket costs. These plans cover about 60% of healthcare expenses.
- **Silver**: Balanced plans that cover about 70% of costs. They may offer more affordable premiums and a reasonable level of cost-sharing.
- **Gold**: These plans cover about 80% of healthcare costs, offering a better level of coverage but higher premiums.
- **Platinum**: The most expensive but also the most comprehensive, covering about 90% of healthcare costs.

How Subsidies Can Help:

- If you qualify for subsidies, these can help lower the monthly premium and reduce your out-of-pocket costs for higher-tier plans.
- **Example**: Without subsidies, a Gold plan may have a premium that is out of reach, but with subsidies, the monthly premium could become much more affordable, and the extra coverage could save you money on healthcare expenses throughout the year.
- ✓ **Action Step**: When comparing plans, consider whether a higher-tier plan (Gold or Platinum) might be more affordable with subsidies, even if the premium is higher. Sometimes, paying a higher

premium may result in **lower overall healthcare costs** due to better coverage and lower co-pays.

How to Avoid Common Mistakes in Selecting a Plan

Choosing a health insurance plan is a personal decision, but there are common pitfalls that many people fall into. Here are some mistakes to watch out for and how to avoid them:

1. Focusing Only on Premiums

- While premiums are an important factor, they shouldn't be the only consideration. A plan with a low premium but a high deductible or high out-of-pocket costs may end up being more expensive in the long run if you need frequent care.

- ✓ **Action Step**: Look at the **total cost of care**, including premiums, deductibles, co-pays, and out-of-pocket maximums. Consider how much you'll likely spend over the year.

2. Not Checking Provider Networks

- Choosing a plan without verifying whether your preferred doctors and hospitals are in-network can lead to surprise costs.

- ✓ **Action Step**: Always check the plan's network list to ensure your doctors and healthcare facilities are covered, particularly if you have ongoing health issues or prefer specific providers.

3. Ignoring Prescription Drug Coverage

➢ Some plans may not cover the medications you need, or they may require you to pay high co-pays for brand-name drugs.

✓ **Action Step**: Verify that your medications are covered under the plan's formulary and compare the costs for prescriptions across different plans.

4. Not Considering Your Healthcare Needs

➢ A low-cost plan may seem appealing, but if it doesn't meet your healthcare needs (e.g., you have a chronic condition or need frequent doctor visits), it might not provide the best value.

✓ **Action Step**: Review your medical history and anticipated healthcare needs for the coming year before selecting a plan.

Understanding Networks, Formularies, and Provider Coverage

When choosing a health plan, it's important to understand the following key terms and how they affect your care:

➢ **Network**: The network is the list of healthcare providers (doctors, hospitals, specialists) that have agreed to provide services at discounted rates under

your plan. Be sure your preferred doctors and hospitals are included in the plan's network.
- **Formulary**: This is the list of prescription drugs covered by the plan. Be sure the medications you take are included and check the cost-sharing arrangement (e.g., generic vs. brand-name drugs).
- **Provider Coverage**: Some plans have coverage restrictions on certain providers or treatments. Check if the plan limits your access to specialists or if you need prior authorization for certain procedures.

Actionable Steps for Maximizing the Value of Your Subsidy

To maximize the value of your subsidy, consider the following steps:

1. **Use the Marketplace Calculator**: This tool can help you estimate your subsidy amount and find plans that fit your budget.
2. **Compare Metal Tiers**: Consider paying a higher premium for a Gold or Platinum plan if subsidies make them affordable.
3. **Factor in All Costs**: Don't just focus on premiums—calculate the total cost of coverage, including co-pays, deductibles, and out-of-pocket maximums.
4. **Check Coverage for Prescriptions and Providers**: Make sure the plan covers your medications and healthcare providers.
5. **Review Your Needs Regularly**: As your healthcare needs change, re-evaluate your plan during each Open Enrollment Period.

Conclusion

Choosing the right health insurance plan is a personal decision that requires careful consideration of your healthcare needs and financial situation. By evaluating plans based on premiums, deductibles, out-of-pocket maximums, and coverage for prescriptions and providers, you can make an informed decision that aligns with your needs. Remember, subsidies can make higher-tier plans more affordable, so don't be afraid to consider more comprehensive coverage if it fits your budget. With careful planning and attention to detail, you can select a plan that offers the best value for you and your family.

Chapter 09

Special Considerations: Families, Seniors, and the Self-Employed

When it comes to healthcare subsidies under the Affordable Care Act (ACA), different groups of people — families, seniors, early retirees, and the self-employed — face unique challenges and opportunities. This chapter will explore these special considerations and provide guidance on how to maximize subsidies based on your specific circumstances. From navigating subsidies for families and dependents to understanding how seniors and self-employed individuals can benefit from ACA provisions, this chapter will help you better understand the rules that apply to your situation and provide actionable steps to make the most of the support available.

Navigating Subsidies for Families and Dependents

Health insurance for families is often more complex than individual plans due to the multiple members involved, each with their own healthcare needs. Fortunately, the ACA provides specific provisions to help make family coverage more affordable, primarily through **Premium Tax Credits (PTC)** and **Cost-Sharing Reductions (CSR)**.

1. Household Size and Income

- ➤ **Eligibility for subsidies** is based not only on income but also on household size. The larger your household, the higher the threshold for eligibility. Subsidies are designed to provide more financial support to families with lower incomes.

> **Example**: A family of four with an income of $80,000 may qualify for subsidies, while a single individual with the same income may not, due to the difference in household size. This is especially important for families with children who are under 18 and are claimed as dependents.

2. Dependent Coverage

> Under the ACA, children can remain on their parent's plan until the age of **26**, which is a key benefit for young adults. However, for families with children under 18, it's important to ensure that all dependents are listed on your health insurance application when applying for subsidies.

✓ **Action Step**: When applying for ACA subsidies, ensure all dependents are included in your household size. Failing to list dependents could result in lower subsidy amounts or ineligibility for subsidies altogether.

3. Special Considerations for Low-Income Families

> Families with very low incomes (e.g., those below 100% of the Federal Poverty Level, or FPL) may qualify for **Medicaid** or **CHIP (Children's Health Insurance Program)**, which can provide even more affordable coverage options. For families with income above 100% FPL but still in the low-to-moderate range, ACA subsidies can provide a

significant reduction in monthly premiums and out-of-pocket costs.

✓ **Action Step**: If your income is below 138% FPL (for Medicaid expansion states), you may qualify for Medicaid, and you should apply through your state's Medicaid program. If you're between 100% and 400% FPL, make sure to explore the **Marketplace** for subsidies.

Subsidy Changes for Seniors and Early Retirees

As individuals transition into retirement or approach age 65, their health insurance needs often change. For seniors and early retirees (those between the ages of 55 and 64), there are important considerations for **subsidy eligibility** and how these individuals can access healthcare coverage before they are eligible for **Medicare** at age 65.

1. Subsidies for Seniors (55-64)

Seniors between the ages of **55 and 64** may qualify for subsidies if their income falls within the 100%-400% of the FPL range. However, because healthcare needs often increase with age, this group can benefit from the ACA's provisions to make healthcare more affordable.

The ACA makes healthcare plans significantly more affordable for seniors in this age group by offering subsidies that offset the higher premiums typically associated with older age.

➢ **Example**: If you are a 58-year-old early retiree with an income of $45,000, you may qualify for subsidies to lower your monthly premiums. Even though insurance premiums rise with age, subsidies can help mitigate those costs.

2. Early Retirees

Many individuals who retire before 65 are not yet eligible for Medicare, so they must secure insurance through the ACA Marketplace or other means. Early retirees may qualify for subsidies based on their household income, which can make ACA plans more affordable.

A common challenge for early retirees is managing the transition from employer-sponsored insurance to individual health insurance. For those who are receiving COBRA coverage (temporary continuation of employer-sponsored coverage), the ACA Marketplace may offer more affordable options, especially if they qualify for subsidies.

➢ **Action Step**: If you're an early retiree, make sure to **compare COBRA coverage** with Marketplace options, especially if you are eligible for subsidies. The Marketplace may offer better coverage options at a lower cost.

3. Medicare Eligibility

➢ Once you turn **65**, you are eligible for Medicare, and you are no longer eligible for ACA subsidies. It's important to plan ahead and transition to Medicare once you become eligible to avoid any gaps in coverage.

✓ **Action Step**: If you are turning 65 soon, make sure to apply for **Medicare** in a timely manner (3 months before your 65th birthday). Also, carefully evaluate **Medicare Advantage** or **Medicare Supplemental** plans for additional coverage.

How the Self-Employed Can Maximize Subsidies Through Accurate Income Reporting

Self-employed individuals face unique challenges when it comes to determining their eligibility for ACA subsidies. Since their income is typically not fixed and may fluctuate from month to month, it's important to accurately report income to the Health Insurance Marketplace to ensure they qualify for the maximum subsidy.

1. Understanding MAGI (Modified Adjusted Gross Income)

The ACA uses **Modified Adjusted Gross Income (MAGI)** to determine subsidy eligibility. MAGI is essentially your **Adjusted Gross Income (AGI)** with specific deductions added back in, such as **tax-exempt interest** and **foreign income**.

For self-employed individuals, MAGI is calculated by taking your business's net profit (income minus business expenses) and adding it to any other sources of income (e.g., interest, dividends).

✓ **Action Step**: To maximize your subsidies, keep accurate records of your business expenses. Deducting allowable business expenses will reduce your taxable income, which in turn will lower your MAGI and potentially increase your eligibility for subsidies.

2. Self-Employment Deductions

➢ The **self-employed health insurance deduction** is one of the key deductions that can reduce your MAGI. If you pay for your own health insurance premiums, you can deduct these expenses from your income, which can significantly reduce the MAGI used to determine your subsidy eligibility.

✓ **Action Step**: Be sure to deduct any **self-employed health insurance premiums** on your taxes, and keep records of your business expenses to lower your MAGI and improve your subsidy eligibility.

3. Fluctuating Income and Seasonality

For many self-employed individuals, income can vary significantly throughout the year, especially if your work is seasonal. For example, if you're a contractor or own a seasonal business, your income may be higher during certain months and lower during others.

It's crucial to report **estimated income for the year** when applying for subsidies. You can estimate your total income based on past years, but be sure to update your application if your income changes significantly.

✓ **Action Step**: If your income fluctuates, you can adjust your subsidy application **mid-year** to reflect changes in your business income. This can help you qualify for higher subsidies during periods of low income.

How to Handle Income Fluctuations (e.g., Seasonal Work, Variable Self-Employment Income)

Self-employed individuals with fluctuating incomes face the challenge of reporting an accurate estimate of their yearly income for ACA subsidies. Whether you have seasonal work or variable income from month to month, it's important to know how to handle these changes.

1. Estimating Annual Income

➤ When applying for ACA subsidies, you'll need to provide an estimate of your **annual income**. For seasonal workers or those with fluctuating income, base this estimate on your previous year's earnings or your expected income for the current year.

- ✓ **Action Step**: Take your most recent tax return and adjust your income for any changes expected during the year, such as fluctuations in business profits or changes in hours worked.

2. Updating Your Income Throughout the Year

- ➤ If your income changes during the year, it's essential to report these changes to the Health Insurance Marketplace. This can increase or decrease your subsidy eligibility.

- ✓ **Action Step**: Log into your Marketplace account and update your income information if you experience significant changes in income. This ensures your subsidy remains accurate, helping you avoid overpaying for premiums or owing a large sum at the end of the year.

3. Managing Large One-Time Income Payments

- ➤ If you receive a large lump-sum payment, such as a business bonus or a one-time payment, it could temporarily push your income above the subsidy threshold.

- ✓ **Action Step**: Report one-time payments separately when estimating your income for subsidies to avoid accidentally exceeding the income limits for subsidies.

Actionable Steps: Special Rules for Families and Self-Employed Individuals

For Families:

- Ensure all dependents are included in your household size.
- If your household income is at or below 400% FPL, apply for subsidies through the Marketplace to lower premiums and out-of-pocket costs.
- If you qualify, consider **Medicaid or CHIP** for children under 18.
- Look for family-friendly plans with good access to pediatric and family care.

For Self-Employed Individuals:

- Use the **self-employment health insurance deduction** to reduce your taxable income and improve your subsidy eligibility.
- Keep accurate income records to determine your **MAGI** and ensure you're reporting your income correctly.
- If your income fluctuates, update your subsidy application **mid-year** to reflect any changes.
- Take advantage of seasonal work by estimating your **annual income** carefully and adjusting as needed.

Conclusion

Navigating ACA subsidies for families, seniors, and the self-employed can seem complicated, but understanding the rules and taking action early can make a significant difference in your healthcare costs. For families, ensuring that all dependents are covered and that you qualify for the maximum subsidies is key. Seniors and early retirees must plan for the transition to Medicare once they turn 65. Self-employed individuals should take care to report income accurately and manage fluctuations effectively to maintain the best possible subsidy eligibility. By following these actionable steps, you can optimize your healthcare coverage and costs for yourself and your family.

Part 4:
The Future of Subsidies and What Lies Ahead

Chapter 10
Policy Shifts: What to Expect in the Coming Years

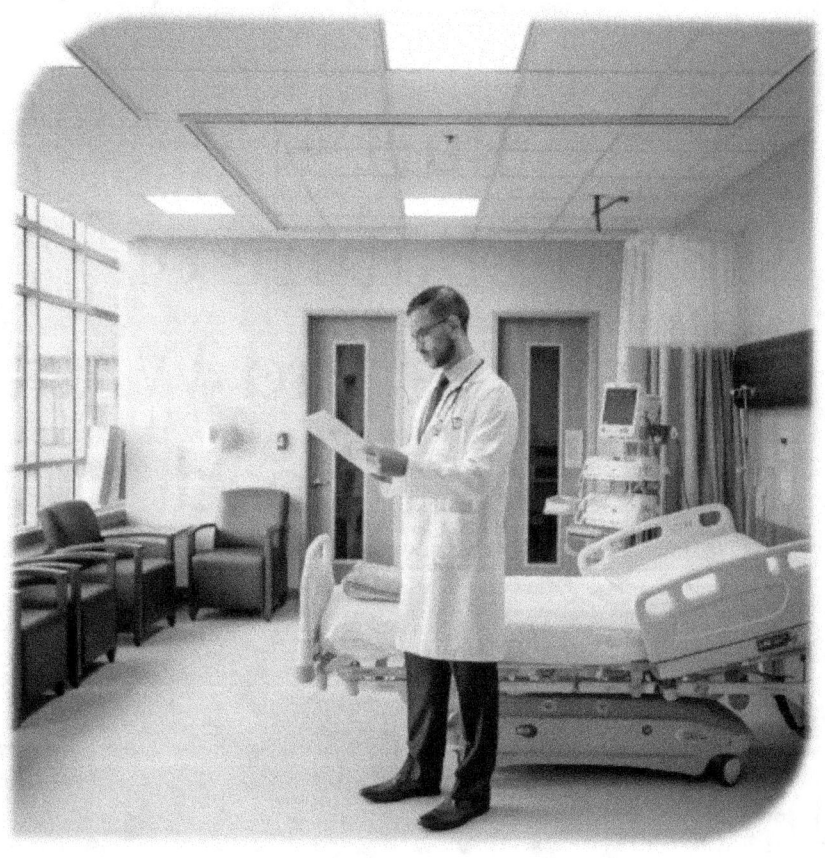

The landscape of healthcare subsidies under the Affordable Care Act (ACA) has been anything but static since its inception. As we look ahead, it's essential to understand the potential policy shifts and reforms that could affect subsidies in the coming years. Whether due to new political administrations, shifts in Congressional priorities, or evolving public health needs, changes to healthcare subsidies are a constant possibility. In this chapter, we will explore the potential changes to subsidies, the likelihood of ACA reforms, and what proposals could alter the future of healthcare in the United States.

Potential Changes to Healthcare Subsidies Under New Political Administrations

Healthcare policy in the U.S. is closely tied to the political landscape, and changes in administration often bring shifts in healthcare priorities. Different political parties have diverse views on healthcare funding, subsidy distribution, and insurance regulations.

1. Democratic Proposals for Expanding the ACA

Expansion of the ACA: Under Democratic leadership, there have been proposals to expand the ACA by increasing subsidies and expanding eligibility. For example, some Democrats have suggested removing the 400% FPL income cap, which currently excludes middle-income earners from receiving subsidies.

Public Option: Another proposal from Democrats is the introduction of a **public health insurance option**. This would create a government-run plan that individuals could opt into as an alternative to private insurance. A public option could help lower costs and increase competition in the Marketplace, potentially driving down premiums for all consumers.

Medicare Expansion: Democratic lawmakers have proposed lowering the eligibility age for **Medicare** from 65 to 60. This would extend coverage to millions of Americans, including those in the 60-64 age group who are particularly vulnerable to high premiums on the Marketplace.

2. Republican Proposals for Reducing Government Involvement

Scaling Back the ACA: On the other side of the political spectrum, Republicans have generally pushed for reducing the scope of government involvement in healthcare. Proposals have included **repealing the individual mandate**, which was effectively eliminated in 2017, as well as **cutting subsidies** or reducing their scope.

Block Grants for Medicaid: Some Republican proposals focus on giving states more control over Medicaid through **block grants**. This would allow states to determine their own eligibility requirements and coverage, potentially resulting in fewer people qualifying for Medicaid and a reduction in coverage options for low-income individuals.

3. Impact of Future Political Shifts

A **Republican-controlled Congress** could lead to cuts or restrictions in subsidies, changes to Medicaid, or attempts to scale back the ACA.

A **Democratic-controlled Congress**, in contrast, may see efforts to expand subsidies, create a public option, or enhance Medicaid eligibility.

✓ **Actionable Step**: Stay informed about the political landscape and follow updates on healthcare legislation. If changes are proposed, understand how they could impact your eligibility for subsidies and premiums.

The Likelihood of ACA Reforms in Congress: A Look at Potential Legislative Actions

While political administrations set the tone for healthcare policy, Congress ultimately passes laws. The likelihood of changes to healthcare subsidies will depend largely on the actions of lawmakers and the priorities of Congress at any given time.

1. Major ACA Reforms: Key Areas of Debate

Income Caps for Subsidies: A key area of reform is whether Congress will consider raising or eliminating the current **income caps for subsidies**. Under the current ACA framework, subsidies are available for individuals and families with incomes between 100% and 400% of the **Federal Poverty Level (FPL)**. Some proposed reforms would extend subsidies to higher-income individuals, while others might seek to reduce subsidy eligibility.

Medicaid Expansion: Medicaid expansion, which was left up to states, remains one of the most debated issues in healthcare reform. As of 2024, **40 states** have adopted Medicaid expansion, but 10 states still have not. Some proposals are pushing for a **national Medicaid expansion**, which would standardize coverage for low-income individuals across all states.

Cost-sharing Reductions (CSRs): Another area of potential reform is CSRs, which reduce out-of-pocket costs for low-income individuals. These payments have been crucial in making Marketplace coverage affordable for many, but their future has been uncertain due to past policy changes and executive actions.

2. Incremental Reforms vs. Overhaul

Incremental Changes: Rather than a complete overhaul, some lawmakers argue for smaller, more gradual reforms to the ACA. These could include adjustments to subsidies, premiums, and eligibility, as well as expanded access to programs like Medicaid or CHIP.

Full Overhaul or Replacement: Alternatively, some legislators advocate for a more sweeping reform of the healthcare system. These proposals range from **Medicare for All**, which would replace private insurance with a government-run program, to other single-payer systems that would provide universal coverage. While these ideas have gained traction, they face significant political opposition.

- **Actionable Step**: Keep track of the proposed healthcare reforms through reliable news sources and be prepared for changes that could affect your subsidy eligibility. Engage in public policy discussions and advocacy to ensure your voice is heard.

How to Prepare for Future Changes in Eligibility or Subsidy Amounts

The future of subsidies will depend on both legislative action and administrative changes. Whether changes are incremental or sweeping, it's crucial to prepare for potential shifts. Here are some ways to ensure you're ready for changes:

1. Monitor Legislative Developments

- **Follow Healthcare News**: Stay informed about changes to the ACA and other healthcare-related policies. Websites like **HealthCare.gov** and major news outlets often provide updates about proposed legislation, changes in eligibility, and shifts in subsidy programs.
- **Contact Your Representatives**: If you have concerns about healthcare policies that affect you,

reach out to your local representatives. Legislators listen to the concerns of their constituents, and you can influence decisions through advocacy.

2. Adjust Your Income and Household Information

Since healthcare subsidies are directly tied to your **household size** and **income**, keeping this information up-to-date on your application is essential. If your income or family size changes, update your Marketplace profile to ensure you're getting the correct subsidy amount.

If you experience significant changes in income due to a job change, divorce, or other life events, be sure to update your Marketplace application promptly to adjust your subsidy eligibility.

3. Explore All Health Insurance Options

- In the future, if ACA subsidies change or are replaced by another program, you may need to explore different health insurance options. Consider alternatives such as **Medicaid, Medicare**, or employer-sponsored plans if you qualify.
- If a **public option** or new government programs emerge, review these options to see if they offer more affordable coverage than the private insurance plans available through the Marketplace.

4. Plan for Potential Cost Changes

Given that healthcare costs tend to rise annually, even with subsidies, it's wise to set aside extra savings to cover future increases in premiums, deductibles, or out-of-pocket costs.

> **Actionable Step**: Budget for potential increases in healthcare expenses and regularly review your health insurance plan during Open Enrollment periods to ensure it still meets your needs and budget.

Exploring New Proposals: Universal Healthcare, Medicare for All, and Beyond

While the ACA has significantly expanded access to healthcare, proposals for more sweeping changes continue to emerge. These include ideas like **Medicare for All, Universal Healthcare**, and other forms of **single-payer systems** that would fundamentally alter how healthcare is delivered and financed in the U.S.

1. Medicare for All

Medicare for All is a proposal that would provide comprehensive healthcare coverage to all Americans, replacing the private insurance market with a **government-run system**. Proponents argue that this would simplify the healthcare system, reduce administrative costs, and expand access to care. However, critics contend that it would raise taxes and reduce the quality of care.

Impact on Subsidies: If a Medicare for All system were implemented, ACA subsidies would likely be phased out, as healthcare would be provided by the government rather than through private insurance plans.

2. Universal Healthcare

Universal healthcare refers to a system where every citizen has access to healthcare services, often funded through taxes. This could take various forms, such as a **single-payer system** or a **multi-payer system**, where private insurers are still involved but regulated by the government.

Impact on Subsidies: Universal healthcare could eliminate the need for ACA subsidies entirely, as healthcare would become a right guaranteed to all citizens, funded by the government. This would be a significant departure from the current system, where subsidies help individuals purchase private health insurance.

> **Actionable Step**: Stay informed about new proposals like Medicare for All or Universal Healthcare and understand how they could change your eligibility for subsidies or access to care. Get involved in policy discussions if you're passionate about healthcare reform.

How to Stay Informed and Involved in Healthcare Policy Discussions

Being proactive in staying informed about healthcare policy changes is crucial for preparing for the future. The healthcare system is constantly evolving, and policy changes can directly affect your access to care and the cost of insurance.

1. Follow Policy Discussions

➢ Subscribe to **healthcare-related news** and policy updates through reputable sources such as **HealthCare.gov**, news outlets, and think tanks focused on healthcare reform.

2. Participate in Advocacy Efforts

➢ Join organizations or grassroots movements that advocate for healthcare policy changes. Whether you support expanding the ACA or pushing for Medicare for All, being involved in advocacy can help ensure that policymakers consider the needs of everyday Americans.

Actionable Steps to Prepare for Future Shifts in Healthcare Subsidies

1. **Monitor legislative changes** and stay updated on potential reforms to the ACA or new proposals like Medicare for All.
2. **Update your Marketplace profile** with accurate income and household information to ensure you're receiving the correct subsidy.

3. **Explore alternative health insurance options**, including Medicaid, CHIP, or employer-sponsored plans, if subsidy eligibility changes.
4. **Advocate for policies** that align with your healthcare needs and stay involved in discussions about healthcare reforms at the national and state level.

By understanding the potential policy shifts and staying proactive about upcoming changes, you can better navigate the evolving landscape of healthcare subsidies and ensure that you're prepared for whatever the future holds. Whether through incremental reforms or more radical changes, your ability to stay informed and take action will help you maintain access to affordable, quality healthcare.

Chapter 11
How to Appeal Denials or Subsidy Adjustments

Healthcare subsidies under the Affordable Care Act (ACA) can make a significant difference in the affordability of health insurance for individuals and families. However, the process of applying for subsidies can sometimes result in denials or unexpected reductions. If your application for subsidies is denied, or if you experience a reduction in your subsidy amount, it's important to know how to effectively navigate the appeals process. In this chapter, we will explore the common reasons for subsidy denials or adjustments, provide a step-by-step guide to appealing decisions, and offer tips for ensuring your subsidy application is accurate and complete. By the end of this chapter, you will have the knowledge to resolve disputes, challenge incorrect decisions, and ensure that you receive the correct amount of financial assistance.

Common Reasons for Subsidy Denials or Reductions

Subsidy denials or reductions are often frustrating, but understanding the common reasons for these issues can help you address the underlying problems and improve your chances of a successful appeal. Below are some of the most frequent causes for denials or reductions:

1. Income Discrepancies

- ➢ One of the most common reasons for subsidy denials is inaccurate or insufficient income reporting. If the Marketplace cannot verify your reported income, it may result in denial of eligibility or a reduction in subsidy amounts. This can happen if you provide

estimates that do not match the IRS or other verification sources.
- Ensure that your **Modified Adjusted Gross Income (MAGI)** is calculated correctly, taking into account all sources of income, including wages, self-employment earnings, investment income, and others.

2. Incorrect Household Size

- Subsidy eligibility is closely tied to the size of your household. If you incorrectly report the number of people in your household or fail to include dependents, it can lead to either a subsidy denial or a lower subsidy amount. It's crucial that your household information is up-to-date and accurate.

3. Missing or Incomplete Documentation

- The ACA Marketplace may request additional documentation to verify income, family size, or other information. Failure to submit required documents on time can lead to delays or denials of your subsidy application.

4. Non-U.S. Citizenship or Immigration Status

- Subsidy eligibility is limited to U.S. citizens, U.S. nationals, or those with legal immigration status. If your application fails to meet these criteria, your subsidy request will likely be denied.

5. Failure to File Taxes

➢ In some cases, individuals who are required to file taxes but do not, or who fail to reconcile advance premium tax credits, may see their subsidy reduced or denied.

6. Changes in Eligibility

➢ If you experience a change in household income, family size, or employment status during the year, your subsidy amount may be adjusted. This can result in a reduction or an increase in your monthly premium assistance.

Step-by-Step Guide to the Appeals Process

If your subsidy application is denied or your subsidy amount is reduced, you have the right to appeal the decision. The appeals process can be complex, but following these steps will help you address the issue efficiently.

1. Review the Denial or Adjustment Notice

Understand the Reason: First, carefully read the notice from the Marketplace explaining the reason for your denial or subsidy adjustment. This will help you determine whether the issue can be corrected or if an appeal is necessary.

Identify the Issue: If your subsidy was reduced or denied, identify whether the issue is related to income verification, household size, immigration status, or another factor.

2. Gather Supporting Documentation

Once you've identified the reason for the denial or adjustment, gather the necessary supporting documents. For example:

- **Income Verification**: Pay stubs, tax returns, W-2s, or bank statements.
- **Household Size**: Birth certificates, tax filings, or custody agreements for dependents.
- **Immigration Status**: Documentation such as a green card, work permit, or U.S. passport.

The more detailed and accurate your supporting documentation, the stronger your appeal will be.

3. Submit a Formal Appeal Request

You can initiate an appeal through the **HealthCare.gov website** or by contacting your state's marketplace if you're in a state with a separate exchange. The appeal process typically involves completing a form or submitting a written request explaining why you believe the subsidy decision was incorrect.

Deadline: Make sure you submit your appeal within the specified timeframe (usually within 90 days of the denial). Missing the deadline may result in the rejection of your appeal.

4. Request a Hearing (If Necessary)

If your appeal is not resolved by documentation alone, you may need to request a **formal hearing** with an appeals officer. In this case, you will have the opportunity to present your case in person or over the phone. An administrative law judge or appeals officer will review your case and make a final determination.

Actionable Step: Prepare for the hearing by reviewing your appeal and supporting documents. Practice explaining your situation clearly and concisely, focusing on the key points that support your case.

5. Wait for the Final Decision

After your appeal is reviewed, you will receive a **final decision** on whether your subsidy eligibility will be reinstated, adjusted, or upheld. If you disagree with the final decision, you can request further review, but this may involve additional steps.

Actionable Step: Be patient during the process, but stay proactive by following up on any delays. Keep copies of all communications and documentation submitted.

How to Effectively Challenge Subsidy Decisions with Documentation

The key to a successful appeal lies in providing clear, complete, and accurate documentation to support your case. Here are some tips for challenging subsidy decisions effectively:

1. Be Clear and Concise

When submitting documentation or explaining your case in an appeal, **be clear and concise**. Clearly state the reason you believe the subsidy decision was incorrect and provide evidence to back up your claims.

Avoid providing extraneous information that may distract from the main issue.

2. Include All Required Documents

- Ensure that all required documents are included in your appeal. Missing documents can delay the process or result in an incomplete appeal. If possible, submit certified copies of documents rather than originals.

3. Highlight Key Information

- In cases where income, family size, or other variables are disputed, **highlight** the key information in your documentation that supports your eligibility for subsidies. For example, if your income was miscalculated, underline or circle the correct figures on your tax forms.

4. Use Official Forms and Channels

- Always use the official forms and communication channels provided by the Marketplace. This ensures that your appeal is processed efficiently and that there are no misunderstandings about your intent.

5. Seek Professional Help if Needed

If your case is particularly complicated, consider seeking help from a **healthcare navigator**, **tax professional**, or **legal expert**. These professionals can guide you through the appeal process, help gather the right documentation, and advocate on your behalf.

> **Actionable Step**: If you're unsure about any aspect of your appeal, seek help from professionals who can ensure your appeal is as strong as possible.

How to Adjust Your Application if You Experience a Change in Income or Family Size

Changes in income or family size can significantly impact your eligibility for subsidies. If you experience such changes, it's important to update your application as soon as possible to ensure that your subsidy amount reflects your new circumstances.

1. Report Income Changes Promptly

> If your income increases or decreases, or if your employment status changes, report these changes to the Marketplace immediately. Delays in reporting income changes can result in overpayment or underpayment of subsidies.

2. Update Household Size

- If you have a child, spouse, or other dependent who joins or leaves your household, make sure to update your Marketplace application to reflect the change. This could lead to an increase or decrease in your subsidy amount.

3. Review Subsidy Adjustments After Major Life Events

- **Life Events**: Major life events like marriage, divorce, the birth of a child, or a job change can affect your subsidy. After such events, review your subsidy eligibility and submit the necessary updates.

4. Use the Marketplace Calculator

The **HealthCare.gov subsidy calculator** can be a helpful tool in determining how changes in income or family size will affect your eligibility for subsidies. It's a good idea to use the calculator before submitting updates to see how the changes may impact your monthly premiums or out-of-pocket costs.

- **Actionable Step**: Keep track of significant life changes throughout the year and update your application in a timely manner to avoid unexpected surprises during tax season.

Understanding "Good Cause" Exceptions for Late or Incomplete Applications

There may be situations where your subsidy application is delayed or incomplete through no fault of your own.

In these cases, the Marketplace may offer **"good cause" exceptions** for late or incomplete applications. Common examples include:

- **Serious illness**: If you were unable to complete your application due to a serious illness.
- **Natural disaster**: If you were affected by a natural disaster, making it difficult to submit your documents on time.
- **Technical errors**: If there were technical issues with the Marketplace website or communication channels.

1. How to Apply for a Good Cause Exception

If you believe you are eligible for a good cause exception, you must explain your situation in writing and provide supporting documentation. For example, a doctor's note may be necessary to prove that a medical condition prevented you from completing your application on time.

Actionable Step: If you believe you qualify for a good cause exception, gather the necessary supporting documents and submit them with your appeal request.

Resolving Disputes and Ensuring Accurate Subsidy Determinations

In the event of a denial or adjustment, resolving disputes and ensuring accurate subsidy determinations requires persistence, clear communication, and timely action. By following the steps outlined in this chapter—gathering accurate documentation, filing timely appeals, and updating your application when necessary—you can significantly improve your chances of receiving the correct amount of financial assistance. If you find yourself in a complicated situation, don't hesitate to seek professional assistance to guide you through the process.

Actionable Steps:

1. **Review** the denial or adjustment notice carefully to identify the cause of the issue.
2. **Gather documentation** that supports your case, such as tax returns, pay stubs, or household documents.
3. **Submit a formal appeal** within the deadline and follow up on your case regularly.
4. **Adjust your application** if your income or family size changes to ensure continued eligibility for subsidies.
5. **Understand good cause exceptions** and apply for them if circumstances beyond your control delayed your application.

By staying proactive and following these steps, you can resolve issues with your healthcare subsidies and ensure that you receive the financial assistance you need to access affordable health insurance.

Chapter 12

The Future of ACA and Healthcare Subsidies: Looking Ahead

As we look toward the future of healthcare in the United States, one of the most critical questions for millions of individuals and families is: **What will happen to healthcare subsidies under the Affordable Care Act (ACA)?** The landscape of healthcare is constantly evolving, and while the ACA has already made significant strides in improving access to affordable coverage, the future of subsidies and health insurance policies remains uncertain. This chapter will explore the long-term sustainability of ACA subsidies, discuss key trends in healthcare, and outline how individuals can influence future healthcare policies. By understanding these dynamics, you'll be better prepared to secure your healthcare future and advocate for a more accessible system.

The Long-Term Sustainability of ACA Subsidies: Will They Continue Beyond 2025?

The ACA subsidies have been instrumental in expanding access to healthcare coverage, especially for low- and middle-income Americans. However, their future beyond 2025 is a topic of ongoing political debate and concern. The following factors will play a major role in determining whether ACA subsidies will continue:

1. Temporary Provisions vs. Long-Term Policy

- **The American Rescue Plan (ARP) and the Inflation Reduction Act (IRA)** have temporarily enhanced ACA subsidies and expanded eligibility for many Americans. These provisions, which were introduced in response to the COVID-19 pandemic, have significantly reduced premiums and out-of-pocket costs for millions of people. However, they are set to expire in 2025 unless Congress takes further action to extend or make them permanent.

➢ **What's at stake?** If these provisions are allowed to expire, millions of Americans could face a sharp increase in their premiums, making health coverage unaffordable once again for many. The question remains: will lawmakers extend or even expand these provisions? Only time will tell, but the ACA subsidy system's future is very much tied to ongoing political decisions.

2. Political Will and Public Opinion

➢ The sustainability of ACA subsidies largely depends on the political will of lawmakers. In recent years, the debate over healthcare policy has been polarized, with differing views on the role of government in healthcare. On one side, many Democrats advocate for expanding and strengthening the ACA, while others push for broader reforms such as **Medicare for All** or universal healthcare.

➢ Public opinion will also play a key role. A broad majority of Americans support affordable healthcare access, and as the impact of subsidies becomes more apparent, especially among middle-income families, pressure on lawmakers to continue or expand subsidies may increase.

3. Potential Challenges to the ACA Subsidy System

➢ Despite the strides made by the ACA, the subsidy system could face several challenges in the future:

✓ **Rising Healthcare Costs:** Healthcare spending continues to grow at unsustainable rates, and if these costs rise faster than subsidies can cover them, many Americans could find themselves priced out of coverage.
✓ **State-Level Variability:** While the federal government has made significant strides in regulating the ACA, some states have either opted out of key provisions (e.g., Medicaid expansion) or are more resistant to ACA reforms, which could leave gaps in coverage or disrupt subsidy availability.

Actionable Step: Keep an eye on **policy proposals** related to healthcare subsidies. Be proactive about reaching out to your representatives to advocate for the continuation of ACA subsidies, particularly the enhanced provisions that have reduced costs for millions.

How ACA Subsidies Have Changed the Healthcare System for Good

Since its implementation, the Affordable Care Act has had a transformative impact on the U.S. healthcare system. One of the ACA's most significant achievements has been the expansion of subsidies, which have allowed millions of people to access affordable health insurance.

Let's examine the positive changes that subsidies have brought to the healthcare system:

1. Expanding Coverage to the Uninsured

➢ Before the ACA, millions of Americans were without health insurance, either because they couldn't afford it or because they had pre-existing conditions that made them uninsurable. ACA subsidies have made it possible for low- and middle-income families to purchase health insurance through the Health Insurance Marketplace, dramatically reducing the number of uninsured Americans.

2. Reducing the Financial Burden of Healthcare

➢ One of the core goals of the ACA was to reduce the financial strain on families caused by high healthcare costs. ACA subsidies have successfully lowered premiums and out-of-pocket costs, allowing people to seek necessary care without the fear of financial ruin. This has been especially impactful for people who previously avoided medical care due to cost concerns.

3. Improving Health Outcomes

➢ With more people insured, healthcare providers have been able to offer more preventive care and early intervention, leading to better health outcomes. Subsidies have particularly benefited people who are at higher risk of chronic conditions by providing access to routine care that can prevent more serious health issues down the road.

4. Creating a More Competitive Market

> By encouraging more people to sign up for health insurance, the ACA has created a larger risk pool, making it easier for insurers to offer competitive rates. This competition has kept premiums lower and improved plan options for consumers.

Actionable Step: If you're currently receiving ACA subsidies, **take advantage** of the system while it's available to you. Regularly review your plan options and ensure you're getting the best value for your premiums.

Key Trends in Healthcare That Will Shape Future Subsidy Policies

The landscape of healthcare in the U.S. is evolving rapidly, and several key trends will likely shape future subsidy policies. These trends will not only affect the affordability and availability of healthcare, but also the types of subsidies individuals may qualify for:

1. The Rise of Value-Based Care

> Traditionally, healthcare providers have been paid based on the volume of services they provide, a model known as **fee-for-service**. However, there is a growing shift toward **value-based care**, where providers are paid based on the quality of care they

deliver and patient outcomes. This shift could lead to lower overall healthcare costs, which may reduce the need for subsidies in the long term, but it could also result in new approaches to how subsidies are structured.

2. Telehealth and Digital Health

- The COVID-19 pandemic accelerated the adoption of telehealth and digital health tools, allowing more people to access healthcare remotely. Telehealth can provide a cost-effective alternative to in-person visits, potentially reducing healthcare costs and making care more accessible to people in rural or underserved areas. Future subsidy policies may need to account for the growing role of telemedicine and how it impacts access to affordable healthcare.

3. Healthcare Inflation and Drug Prices

- Healthcare inflation, particularly around prescription drug prices, remains a key concern for the future of ACA subsidies. If the cost of medications and treatments continues to rise, subsidies will need to be adjusted to ensure that individuals can still afford care. This could lead to new policy proposals to control healthcare inflation or cap out-of-pocket costs for drugs.

4. Shift Toward Preventive Care

- There is an increasing focus on preventive care to reduce long-term healthcare costs. Policies that encourage healthy lifestyles, disease prevention, and early detection are likely to be prioritized in the future. This could lead to adjustments in subsidy eligibility to incentivize people to enroll in wellness programs or take advantage of preventive services.

Actionable Step: Stay informed about healthcare trends and how they might affect the availability and design of subsidies. If you are involved in an industry that intersects with healthcare, consider advocating for policies that promote the sustainability of the ACA and its subsidy system.

Moving Toward More Affordable, Accessible Healthcare Options

The ultimate goal of the ACA and healthcare subsidies is to make healthcare more affordable and accessible for all Americans. Moving forward, several reforms could help ensure this goal is met:

1. Expansion of Medicaid

➤ The ACA's Medicaid expansion allowed states to extend coverage to more low-income individuals, but not all states have participated. In the future, there may be greater efforts to push for universal Medicaid expansion, allowing more people to access affordable care.

2. Public Option

➢ The concept of a **public option**—a government-run insurance plan that competes with private insurers—has gained traction in recent years. If enacted, a public option could lower premiums and provide a more affordable alternative for consumers, especially if ACA subsidies are not enough to meet rising healthcare costs.

3. Standardized Plan Options

➢ Standardized plans that offer similar coverage at different price points could simplify the process of comparing health insurance options and help consumers make more informed decisions. This would also increase transparency and potentially make it easier for people to choose the most affordable plan based on their needs.

Actionable Step: If you feel that **healthcare affordability** is a significant issue, get involved in local or national **advocacy groups** pushing for healthcare reforms. Your voice can help shape policies that move toward more affordable healthcare for all.

How Individuals Can Influence the Future of Healthcare Subsidies Through Advocacy and Participation

The future of ACA subsidies isn't just determined by policymakers in Washington, D.C. Individuals, families, and communities can have a significant influence on the direction of healthcare policies through active participation and advocacy:

1. Engage with Policymakers

- Reach out to your local representatives and senators to voice your support for continued or expanded subsidies. Participate in town hall meetings, write letters, and stay informed about legislative efforts related to healthcare.

2. Participate in Public Comment Periods

- Many proposed healthcare reforms, including changes to the ACA, go through public comment periods where citizens can submit feedback. Take advantage of these opportunities to make your voice heard.

3. Join Advocacy Organizations

- Organizations like **Families USA** and **the Center on Budget and Policy Priorities** work tirelessly to ensure that healthcare subsidies remain robust and accessible. Joining these groups can help amplify your voice and connect you with others who share your concerns.

Actionable Step: Stay involved by **signing petitions**, attending rallies, or even becoming a part of advocacy groups that fight for better healthcare policies. It's important to make sure lawmakers know that affordable healthcare remains a top priority for the American people.

Final Action Steps: What You Can Do Now to Secure Your Healthcare Future

In summary, the future of healthcare subsidies will depend on ongoing political decisions, economic factors, and the ability of individuals to engage in meaningful advocacy. To secure your healthcare future, consider the following action steps:

- **Review your current healthcare plan** and ensure that it aligns with your needs.
- **Stay informed** about potential changes to ACA subsidies and how they may impact your healthcare costs.
- **Advocate for continued and expanded subsidies** through communication with your representatives and participation in public discussions.
- **Plan for the future** by considering alternatives like the **public option** or **Medicaid expansion** if available in your state.

By taking these steps, you can ensure that you remain prepared for any changes in the healthcare system and can continue to access affordable health coverage no matter what the future holds.

This concludes the final chapter of the guide, giving you a comprehensive understanding of the future of ACA subsidies and actionable steps to secure your healthcare future.

Conclusion

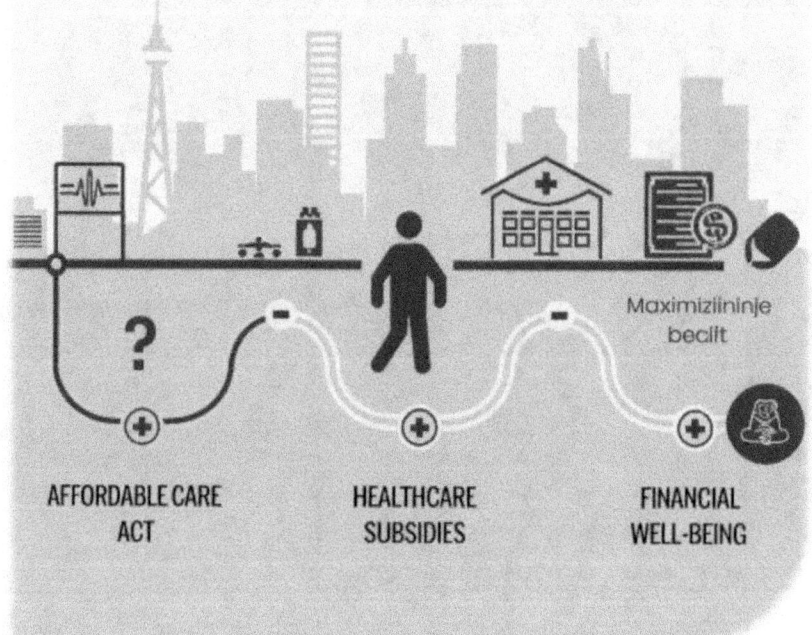

Charting Your Path Forward

Navigating the complexities of healthcare subsidies can feel overwhelming, but understanding the key elements of the Affordable Care Act (ACA) and staying informed about changes will empower you to make the most of the resources available to you. In this guide, we've explored the foundations of healthcare subsidies, the recent changes that have reshaped the landscape, and practical strategies for maximizing your benefits. Now, as we wrap up, it's time to reflect on the key takeaways and chart your path forward to secure your health and financial well-being in the years to come.

Recap of Key Takeaways for Navigating Healthcare Subsidies

The ACA and its subsidies have provided a lifeline to millions of Americans, helping them access the healthcare they need without financial hardship. However, the system is constantly evolving. Here are the key takeaways to keep in mind:

Healthcare subsidies are designed to make insurance more affordable, based on your income and family size. They reduce monthly premiums and out-of-pocket costs, allowing more people to access necessary medical care.

Eligibility for subsidies is tied to income and household size. The Federal Poverty Level (FPL) is the primary factor, and various enhancements over the years (like those from the American Rescue Plan and

Inflation Reduction Act) have temporarily expanded access to subsidies, even for those above 400% FPL.

The Health Insurance Marketplace is the primary tool for applying for and comparing plans that include subsidies. Understanding how to navigate it—whether through HealthCare.gov or a state-based exchange—can significantly reduce your healthcare costs.

Changes to the ACA and subsidy policies are inevitable, especially as emergency measures like the American Rescue Plan's enhancements are set to expire in 2025. Staying informed about legislative actions and participating in healthcare policy discussions will help you adapt to these changes.

Maximizing subsidies requires careful attention to plan details. Comparing premiums, deductibles, and out-of-pocket costs across different plans ensures that you're getting the best value. Consider using the Marketplace's tools to estimate your potential subsidy and plan options.

The Ongoing Importance of Staying Informed About ACA Changes

The world of healthcare subsidies is not static. As demonstrated throughout this guide, changes in the ACA are not only driven by political factors but also by economic shifts, public health needs, and technological advancements.

Why Staying Informed Matters:

Policy Changes: Legislative changes, such as those brought about by the Inflation Reduction Act or proposed modifications to ACA subsidies, can dramatically affect your eligibility and financial obligations. Staying informed ensures that you don't miss out on benefits or face unexpected cost increases.

New Proposals: Healthcare reform is a hot topic in Washington, and proposals like the public option, universal healthcare, or even changes to Medicaid expansion could reshape the future of healthcare subsidies. Keeping abreast of these changes gives you the chance to participate in discussions and advocate for policies that align with your needs.

Annual Adjustments: Each year, subsidy eligibility thresholds and plan details are updated. By keeping track of these changes, you can be proactive in reviewing your health plan and making necessary adjustments to maintain or increase your coverage.

How to Stay Informed:

- Sign up for updates on **HealthCare.gov** or your state exchange website.
- Follow healthcare-related news through reliable sources like **Kaiser Family Foundation (KFF)**, **Health Affairs**, and **The Centers for Medicare and Medicaid Services (CMS)**.
- Stay engaged with advocacy groups, such as **Families USA** or **The National Public Health Association**, which often provide updates

on proposed changes and opportunities for public input.

Practical Advice for Maintaining Coverage and Maximizing Subsidies

Taking full advantage of the ACA's subsidies requires proactive effort. To ensure that you maintain affordable coverage and get the most out of your subsidies, here are some practical steps to consider:

1. Review Your Coverage Regularly

Your healthcare needs will evolve, and so will the plans available to you. Review your plan each year during the **Open Enrollment Period** to make sure you're still getting the best deal for your situation. Don't assume that last year's plan will continue to be the best choice.

- Look at factors such as **premium increases**, changes in provider networks, and coverage for medications and specialist care.
- If you experience life changes, such as a marriage, job loss, or income fluctuation, make sure to **update your Marketplace application** so you don't lose eligibility for subsidies.

2. Be Strategic About Plan Selection

When comparing plans in the Marketplace, consider your **healthcare usage** and your ability to pay both **premiums** and **out-of-pocket costs**. Subsidies may lower premiums, but they don't cover everything. Be sure to consider:

- **Doctor access**: Make sure your preferred doctors are in-network.
- **Prescription coverage**: Check that the medications you need are covered under the plan's formulary.
- **Out-of-pocket maximums**: Understand how much you would have to pay in case of an emergency or significant medical event.

3. Understand Your Tax Credit and Cost-Sharing Reductions

The subsidy system includes two main components: **Premium Tax Credits (PTC)** and **Cost-Sharing Reductions (CSR)**. These are different financial aids that lower your premiums and out-of-pocket costs. Make sure you understand how they work and their implications for your overall healthcare spending:

- **Premium Tax Credit (PTC)**: This is the subsidy that lowers your monthly premium costs based on your income.
- **Cost-Sharing Reduction (CSR)**: This is a subsidy that reduces the amount you pay for deductibles, copayments, and coinsurance.

If you're eligible for both PTC and CSR, be sure to apply for both when you apply for coverage.

Encouragement to Advocate for Continued Improvements in Healthcare Access

While healthcare subsidies have helped millions, the fight for truly affordable healthcare is far from over. The ACA has made great strides, but it's important to continue advocating for policies that can improve healthcare access for everyone, especially the most vulnerable groups.

How You Can Advocate for Change:

- **Reach out to Your Representatives:** Write letters, make calls, or attend town hall meetings to voice your support for maintaining or expanding subsidies. Politicians need to hear from their constituents about the importance of affordable healthcare.
- **Join Advocacy Groups:** Whether through local organizations or national efforts, your involvement can help amplify the demand for accessible healthcare. Groups like **Families USA** and **The Center on Budget and Policy Priorities** work tirelessly to protect and enhance healthcare subsidies.
- **Stay Educated on Policy Proposals:** Learn about the latest healthcare proposals, such as **Medicare for All** or the **public option**, and join the conversation about how these changes could impact you and others.

Final Thoughts on Achieving Long-Term Health and Financial Well-Being Through Strategic Use of Subsidies

Healthcare subsidies have made a world of difference in the lives of millions, but the future of healthcare affordability will ultimately depend on how we engage with and shape the healthcare system going forward.

Here's how you can secure your healthcare future:

- **Be proactive**: Understand how subsidies work, regularly review your health plan, and make adjustments as needed.
- **Stay informed**: Keep up to date with the latest changes to healthcare policies and subsidies.
- **Advocate**: Be vocal about the importance of affordable healthcare, and participate in shaping the policies that affect you and your community.

By taking these steps and remaining engaged, you can ensure that you and your loved ones continue to have access to high-quality, affordable healthcare for years to come. Healthcare is an essential part of your long-term well-being—both physical and financial—and with the right tools and information, you can maximize the subsidies available to you and chart a path toward a healthier, more secure future.

This concludes our guide on navigating changes in the Affordable Care Act and healthcare subsidies. We hope this book has empowered you to make informed decisions and take meaningful action in securing your healthcare coverage.